AXIOLOGICAL ETHICS

Axiological Ethics

J. N. FINDLAY, F.B.A.

Clark Professor of Moral Philosophy and Metaphysics, Yale University

MACMILLAN
ST MARTIN'S PRESS

© J. N. Findlay 1970

First published 1970 by
MACMILLAN AND CO LTD
London and Basingstoke
Associated companies in New York Toronto
Dublin Melbourne Johannesburg and Madras

SBN (paper) 333 00269 5

Printed in Great Britain by
RICHARD CLAY (THE CHAUCER PRESS) LTD
Bungay Suffolk

170
F 493

CONTENTS

61207

EDITOR'S PREFACE

Professor Findlay writes in this monograph: 'There really is, it would seem, an organised framework of values and disvalues within which our practical decisions must be made, and philosophy must give some account of the structure of this framework and of the principles guiding its construction.' He attempts to meet the philosophical need referred to in two ways. The views of some of the most important axiological thinkers are clearly and critically expounded. To this exposition the author adds his own opinions about value-theory.

The names of the authors to whom Professor Findlay refers are well known, but, with the exception of G. E. Moore, their writings are not now widely read, at any rate in places where analytical philosophy flourishes. Professor Findlay deplores this state of affairs. He considers, for example, that we should profit at least as much from a close study of the later chapters of Moore's *Principia Ethica* which make him 'one of the prime founders of axiology' as we do from our close study of the earlier chapters on the naturalistic fallacy which have made Moore 'the father of modern meta-ethics'. Whether the reader would agree with that or not, he will be most grateful for the clarity and learning with which the author of this monograph presents axiological ethics. He will find the pages which follow characteristically lively, forthright, readable and provocative.

Professor Findlay's exploration of this branch of ethics will guide students who know nothing of axiological ethics deftly through territory into which they might otherwise be deterred from venturing. Those readers who are familiar with this field will be particularly interested in the author's attempt to construct a value-theory of his own.

The University of Exeter   W. D. HUDSON

I. INTRODUCTION

The aim of this monograph is to study a strand of ethical enquiry which has been present throughout the history of ethical thought, but which has in fairly recent times been given an independent development and has thereby illuminated the whole field of ethical questions. Axiology or Value-Theory began as a tailpiece to Ethics, but it arguably ought to end as the tail which wags the dog, which by illuminating the ends of practice alone makes the prescription of norms for practice itself a practicable undertaking. This monograph will study the thought of those who have done most to detach value-theory as a discipline from the practical enquiries in which it had its origin, and on which it in its turn can be used to throw light.

The word 'axiology' (like the more Germanic 'value-theory') is probably still felt to be barbaric by the best philosophical speakers in England: its value, however, lies in demarcating an enquiry, of great importance and illumination, which will probably not be explored, if its boundaries with other disciplines remain confused and blurred. The word 'axiology' was introduced into philosophy by Urban in 1906 in his heavily excellent book *Valuation: Its Nature and Laws*: it was used to translate the *Werttheorie* which the Austrian economist von Neumann had introduced into economics, and which the Austrian philosophers Ehrenfels and Meinong, concerned at all costs to follow the lead of 'science', had tried to cultivate in the field of aesthetic, moral, scientific and other values. 'Axiology' meant the study of the ultimately worthwhile things (and of course of the ultimately counterworthwhile things) as well as the analysis of worthwhileness (or counterworthwhileness) in general. Urban's book, with its elaborately stated theory of 'affective-conative meaning' was a valuable introduction of the thought-trends of Brentano, Meinong and Ehrenfels to English-speaking thinkers, and possibly a remote inspirer of the less well elaborated theories of 'emotive meaning' held later in the century by Ogden, Richards and Stevenson. Axiology, like other similar European movements, flourished faintly beyond the Atlantic, inspiring such interesting developments as Perry's behaviouristic *General Theory of Value* (1926) and Brogan's good papers on 'betterness' as the fundamental value-universal. Meanwhile, on the continent, the enquiry into value passed beyond the abstract stage represented by Lessing's work on *Wertaxiomatik* and some posthumously published work of Husserl's, and became interested in wider questions of the good life in general, and its relation to the norms of conduct which played such a preponderant role in traditional ethics. There were produced two immensely valuable systematic studies of the whole realm of values and the principles underlying its institution: Max Scheler's *Der Formalismus in der Ethik und die materiale Wertethik* (*Formalism in Ethics and the Material Value-Ethic*) (1916), and Nicolai Hartmann's *Ethik* (*Ethics*) (1926), translated into English by Stanton Coit in 1932. These are works which not only ask what worthwhileness and counterworthwhileness may be in general, but to what in detail they apply, and that not by arbitrary imposition, but in virtue of their inner sense and content. With them may be compared the British delineations of the value-realm found in G. E. Moore (especially in the last, little-read chapters of *Principia Ethica*, 1903), in Hastings Rashdall (*The Theory of Good and Evil*, 1907), and in considerable parts of W. D. Ross's *The Right and the Good* (1930) and *The Foundations of Ethics* (1939). It is with these foundational works, British and continental, that the present monograph will be mainly concerned.

The years since the initial launching and flowering of axiology have involved a profound set-back for it as for all branches of traditional philosophising. The star of Wittgenstein rose in the British and that of Heidegger in the continental firmament, and the blaze of these luminaries was temporarily such as to render the whole constellated pattern of traditional and recent problems and findings invisible. Wittgenstein thought in terms of a programme designed to bring words back from their elaborate and philosophical, to their most ordinary, commonplace uses, and in terms of such a programme talk about values and their relations became nothing but an inflated, misleading surrogate for the commendatory, prescriptive talk of ordinary life. It was this that must be studied and clarified, in a 'meta-ethical' rather than a straightforwardly ethical perspective. On the continent, likewise, Heidegger, with his determination to see all things only in the light of an agonised, barely expressible personal subjectivity, made short work of the edifices raised by the systematic value-theorists. At the level at which Heidegger's existential person lives and confronts the world and society, there can be no values in any organised, systematically discussable sense, only the tortured preferences of the individual, into whose loneliness, styled 'authenticity', the whole organised world of value and being has been absorbed. Both Wittgenstein and Heidegger emerged upon the disintegrated middle-European scene of 1918 onwards in the form of disintegration made conscious and systematic. Their utterances acted as an immense blanketing snowfall beneath which the whole pattern of ordered philosophical discourse lay for a time buried. In the hope of many, including the author of the present monograph, this snowfall is at present in process of vanishing more or less tracelessly, leaving only some extremely illuminating changes in matter and method to diversify the philosophical landscape. These large issues cannot, however, be argued in the present context.

Axiology is therefore the product of a fairly recent period in thought-history which, temporarily overwhelmed by a general disturbance, now bids fair to remain, in its essential 'problematic', a permanent field for philosophising. All this must not be taken to mean that axiology is basically a new thing, that it is not part and parcel of the whole tradition of philosophy. It has always existed, though largely subordinated to the discipline of ethics, the investigation of what ought to be done, or of what it is that something ought to be done. What is worthwhile *per se* or the contrary is, of course, something having the closest possible relation to what ought to be done, but nevertheless not so close as not to leave it possible to assert the existence or possibility of worthwhile or unworthwhile things having little or no relation to what ought to be done. The field of ethics certainly presupposes the field of axiology, but the latter, arguably, stretches out beyond the limits of the former. The relations between the worthwhile and the practically demanded are obviously of that deep, puzzling kind which form the basic material of philosophy – relations where identities suddenly show gulfs and where gulfs abridge themselves to identities – and cannot be further considered here. Suffice it to say that the concepts work differently, and are not in any simple manner interchangeable, and that it is not a service to philosophy to treat the one solely in relation to the other.

That axiology flourished among the Greeks is shown by the frequently uttered but untrue complaint that they had no concept corresponding to the modern notion of obligation. It is also shown in the well-known complaint against the Platonic Socrates that he professes a sort of 'ideal utilitarianism', in which doing as one ought is in a subtle manner *confused* with having what is worthwhile, so that being a practitioner of virtue comes to be identified with a sort of personal profit, which then assorts strangely with the ordinary personal profit of good birth, fortune, wealth, etc., and the vanishing delights of the senses. The Platonic Socrates, it is plain, is trying to cozen us into following a right way of life, and into ordering our souls correctly, by persuading us that such correctness of life and behaviour is an intrinsically worthwhile thing, and that not merely for some outside judge but for ourselves who live in this manner. And Plato emancipated from Socrates is plainly more concerned to give us an axiological hierarchy than a set of ethical precepts: thus the *Philebus* teaches us to accord supreme value to the Measure or Limit from which all excellence and all beauty derive, and secondary value to the various specifications of such Measure or Limit, while the mind and wisdom which acquaint us with such values are valuable in a third degree, the sciences and arts in a fourth and the pure pleasures which accompany the sciences and certain uses of the senses in a fifth and last degree. It is in terms of these values that our life should be shaped, and Plato is much more clear as to the factors that enter into the shaping than as to the precise, right compromise that governs their combination. If we turn to Aristotle we have a similar overweight of axiology over ethics. No question is in fact raised as to the propriety of an action or a way of living other than its subservience to a single supreme end of welfare or happiness, into whose concept, however, many distinct factors are fitted. And the subsequent history of Stoicism and Epicureanism illustrates the conflict in axiological theory of contents which are not merely both good, but good *in different ways*: both systems were, however, wedded to an axiomatic monism which meant that only one of these ways could be genuine.

If we now move to the eighteenth century, we certainly find problems of axiology equally stressed with problems of conduct or ethics. Thus Richard Price whose main concern is to prove that 'we express necessary truth when we say of some actions that they are right and of others that they are wrong' (Selby-Bigge, *British Moralists*, Clarendon Press, 1897; Bobbs-Merrill reprint, 1964, para. 616), none the less also says that 'it is not possible to contemplate and compare dead matter and life, brutality and reason, misery and happiness, virtue and vice, ignorance and knowledge, impotence and power, the deity and inferior beings, without acquiring the ideas of better and worse, perfect and imperfect, noble and ignoble, excellent and base' (Selby-Bigge, para. 640). Similarly if we turn to Hutcheson we have not only the clearly set-forth distinction of 'natural' and 'moral' good, but a variety of 'senses' acquainting us with what can only be called a series of disparate values: the agreeable and the disagreeable, the aesthetic values resident in 'uniform objects', as well as the moral values proportioned, in axiomatic fashion, to the benevolence, the ability, and the private good achieved or sacrificed by the agent (Selby-Bigge, paras 126, 127). In Kant, likewise, we have a deeply involved mixture of the ethical and the axiological, despite the widely held view that he is only concerned to specify a law or principle for rational action and not to put before us any material end to endeavour. Kant moves from laying down the Categorical Imperative in its first form, as a pure guide to ethical action, to the axiological principle that sees in the will which follows the Categorical Imperative the only unconditionally worthwhile thing in the world. Only a very confused intelligence can imagine that acting on universalisable maxims and respecting the will which so acts are in any way identical or even logically equivalent postures: a stout ethical purist might in fact forbid any idolatrous reverence for the will which conforms to the moral law. In the same way, there are many infusions of the axiological into Kantian imperativism, in the command, for example, to treat persons as absolute ends, in the belief that a Divine Agent will apportion happiness to virtue, as also in various cognitive and aesthetic valuations which meet us throughout the Kantian writings. Kant is in fact much nearer to setting up a comprehensive material ethic of values than Scheler and other critics have supposed. And if, finally, we turn from Kant to the Utilitarians we see there too an unquestioned stress on a simplified axiology, in which all values and disvalues are concentrated into the positive end of pleasure and the negative end of avoidance of pain. This axiology is combined with an imperfect ethic in which, under the guise of estimating quantities of pleasure and pain, we in effect say how we must decide among different cases of pleasure and pain. What we have said has made plain that questions of ultimate worthwhileness and counterworthwhileness have been as much part of the warp and woof of traditional ethical theory as more narrowly conceived discussions of what ought to be done.

We shall now, in the rest of this introductory chapter, clarify some linguistic and conceptual issues, and some questions of principle, which will at least prepare us for the field of views and problems that we are about to consider. We shall employ the term 'value' as a philosophical equivalent of the goodness, the excellence, the desirability and what not which we attribute to certain sorts of objects, states and situations: such value is very plainly correlated, and correlated in principle, with attitudes that we shall call 'valuations', for which well-established philosophical term 'cherishing', 'setting store by', 'esteeming', 'prizing', 'having a pro-attitude towards' may serve as ordinary or new-fangled equivalents. The circumscription of 'valuation' or 'cherishing' will concern us later: for the time being it is sufficiently clear what these terms cover, though it is worth stressing that not every passing tinge of agreeable feeling inspired by a situation amounts to a valuation or involves an attribution of value, but only one that represents a moderately stable posture of soul, and to some extent also wishes its object to *exist*, to be a stable part of the world.

It is further clear that valuation, however evanescent, is necessarily consequent on some character or specification which is capable of being distinguished from the value we find in an object, and which is what we value an object *for*, our reason for finding it precious, etc., such a character or specification being in principle such as could be elsewhere and otherwise exemplified. Even when individuals are valued for being the individuals they are, there is an obscure reference to specifications they fulfil, and occasions on which these specifications are manifest, or at least to occasions on which they can be repeatedly contemplated or assessed. Valuation clearly has a built-in generality, even if there are special problems concerned with the undoubtedly genuine valuation of individuality and of particular individuals. This built-in generality of valuations however makes it natural and proper to speak of 'a value' or of 'values' in the plural, where a value means an association of value with a particular character or specification which really reflects the valuation of a given person or set of persons, e.g. justice, Norman lineage or sportsmanship are for some persons 'values'. It is artificial, and likewise question-begging, to refer to such things merely as 'grounds of value', suggesting that valuation and value should be something amorphous and undifferentiated and externally wedded to the make-up and character of objects, whether in human experience or in reality. The so-called 'descriptive content' which can be clearly separated from the 'evaluative meaning' which seems to penetrate it may be a valuable philosophical distinction at certain levels of abstraction. It does not follow that it is so at all such levels.

Beside 'values' and 'valuations' we must of course never forget to range 'disvalues' and 'disvaluations', little as we may care for the latter pair of terms. Disvaluation covers the rejection, the spurning, the reproving and disapproving of some state or content, a rejection likewise fairly stable in character and directed to some more or less stable existence or non-existence in the actual world. It is of supreme importance that in axiological considerations we should never assume that disvalues are in any sense the mirror-image of values, that the absence of goodness is automatically very bad, or the absence of badness deeply good, etc., or that the principles governing valuation and disvaluation are in any way closely parallel.

Values and disvalues, and the attitudes connected with them, must likewise obviously admit of comparativeness or degree. A scale or scales of degrees tending to a vague 'infinity' in either direction and passing through a common centre of 'indifference', is plainly part and parcel of our subject-matter. We must not, however, assume that values and disvalues always permit of such scalar comparison, and we must also recognise the complexities introduced by certain quasi-values which are merely the shadows of contrary disvalues. All these points will concern us later.

'Values' and 'valuations' must further, it is plain, permit of a distinction, not always wholly clear, but certainly always felt even by moderately sophisticated persons, between such values and valuations as are freely allowed to be 'personal', peculiar to the individual, and neither expected nor required to hold for other persons, and other valuations and values which are felt to impose themselves with a certain necessity or ineluctability, which it is felt must impress itself on *anyone*, or at least on anyone who reflects at all carefully on the matter. Thus the valuation of sitting on beaches or eating meals in the open or wearing flowers in one's hair are obviously by their very nature and structure matters on which no agreement can be expected or demanded, whereas the valuation of being happy, of enjoying freedom and power, even of triumphing over one's adversaries, of being truly informed as to the state of things, etc., are obviously, in varying degrees, values disagreement with which tends to seem absurd, unfeasible, perverse, mistaken, wrong. (These seemings may, of course, as in the fourth case, seem open to correction.) Our impression may be mistaken, but the utterances 'I like bondage, I rejoice in being discriminated against, I value a state of deep unhappiness' seem

8

to involve a certain deep absurdity comparable to saying that A is a C because it does *not* belong to certain classes of things which are Cs. Such things can be said, they are not even formally self-contradictory, but they involve a certain vein of deep nonsense of which philosophy must take account. And while this nonsense is less evident in cases that involve *others*, the very notion of valuing things differently merely because they apply to others, seems in a deep sense arbitrary and nonsensical. Between these extreme limits of values and valuations which seem to have a cogent and mandatory quality and others which have no such character, lies a whole spectrum of intermediate cases, those which in a vague manner impress us as mandatory and cogent but in whose case we can readily be brought to doubt their cogent or mandatory character. All these distinctions are genuinely 'part of the phenomena', whether or not we decide that they can ultimately be sustained.

Valuation and values stand further, with great obviousness, as previously mentioned, in relation to various requirements, exigencies, demands, imperatives, which are most readily expressed by some case of the auxiliary verb 'ought' or 'should'. These exigencies are experienced by ourselves, and are also brought home to others, by certain manifest attitudes which can, on the one hand, be regarded as forms of valuation, though they may equally, on the other hand, be regarded as merely related phenomena. They are attitudes marked by an urgency, a dynamic pressure, which are characteristic of some, but not all manifest cases of valuation. These 'oughts' and 'shoulds' are, as has been often pointed out, as various in type as the valuations or disvaluations to which they are related: some are serious, some playful, some personal, some full of soidisant mandatoriness, some identified with a peculiar group or community, some seeming to voice the feeling of all men without restriction. Some are as much matters of degree, as much affected with comparativeness, as are certain valuations which correspond to them. There are, however, others which have a certain summary, all-or-none character which makes them quite different from valuations. That A ought to be B and ought on no account to be C, represent pure exigencies from which the value-content has,

9

as it were, been emptied out: it is only when we enquire into the why of such impressions that value-content comes back into the picture. And the most purely summary or all-or-none of these 'oughts' or 'shoulds' are plainly the ethical 'oughts' or 'shoulds', the 'oughts' or 'shoulds' of our most serious social practice. These are not matters of degree, since whatever the importance or lack of importance of the values which condition choice or action, choice and action themselves admit no degree: one must either do or not do something. An alternative B may be nearly as choiceworthy as A, but in the actual choice the doing of A may mean the total omission of B. Not all action, however, is dominated by an ethical 'ought', and, where none is present, arbitrary preference, perhaps guided by values, personal or mandatory, takes over.

What we have so far said has sketched the main distinctions in the field of valuation and their relation to other distinctions and to one another. We have accepted a technical language because it has seemed to us to do better justice to the working of our ordinary terms and concepts in this field than the language of liking, approving, caring for, setting store by, preferring, etc., with its innumerable shifts and transitions. Philosophy must decide what distinctions are philosophically worth drawing, and while respectful to ordinary usage, particularly in the initial pinning down of its notions, it must remain magisterial in its final use of them. And a new philosophical usage can successfully hit off a distinction we wish to draw, basing itself on its own philosophical sense of ease or unease, without necessarily deferring to *non*-philosophical ease or disquiet. We have now to consider the main problems which the distinctions just drawn readily provoke, and to which the philosophers we are due to study gave very different answers.

The first and most fundamental question which an axiological ethics must confront is plainly that of the nature of the valuation, the setting store by something, which is also plainly a clearer, more graspable thing than the 'value' with which, under its influence, objects are 'credited' by us. Is this valuation primarily a stance which *we*, as agents or experients, take up to objects or states which come before us, or is it primarily a 'light' in which objects or states appear before us, much as they come before us as being about to do this or that, or as having this or that bearing on one another, etc.? In other words, is valuation primarily an attitudinal or a phenomenological matter, a matter of how someone stands to some content or a matter of the *way* in which that content comes up or appears before him? Or is there both an attitudinal and a phenomenological side to the matter, and is there perhaps some deep relation between them? We shall see that Meinong, for example, has much to say on these matters. And if we now turn to the attitudinal side of valuation, there is a question unasked by the philosophers in our purview as to whether attitudes are to be studied as *behaviour*, in the form they take for an outside observer, or in the 'inward' form they take for the man who has them, or perhaps in both forms conjointly, and perhaps without according primacy to either. And there is the further, central question as to whether, in considering the attitudinal side of valuation, we shall lay stress on the element of *striving* for or against the realisation of something, which some have made crucial to valuation, or on the element of emotional appraisal, positive or negative, which to others has seemed equally crucial, or, lastly on some deliberate openness to the phenomena of the value-sphere by which all such emotions and practical responses are in some way provoked or triggered off. Is valuing primarily being ready to have wants, being ready to have feelings or being simply open to see things in certain 'lights'? This leads us on to consider the other side of valuation, the nature of the 'light' in which a valued object comes before us, as precious, as worthy of admiration, etc., a light which is often more evident to the valuing person than any attitude he may have to an object, and which can persist and haunt him even when the relevant attitude is quite in abeyance. Philosophers may dilate on the absurdity of attributing values to things instead of connecting them with our own reactions, but the fact remains that our own reactions are not the locus where they often appear to be: they seem to inform, to pervade, to be modally attached to objects or states of affairs. The world of our normal experience is not the neutral world of the impartial scientist: it is painted with as many axiological tinges as men have sentiments. We have therefore to consider how best to describe the tinges in question. Are they analysable in terms of some obscure readiness to evoke attitudes in persons? Or in terms of some not further analysable but relational modality of 'fitness' or 'fittingness'? Or in terms of some wholly unanalysable, simple predicate or quality? All these questions and many more have been explored by the axiologists of our period, but by none more conscientiously than Alexius Meinong in the various treatises we shall consider later. What it is important to stress is that none of these questions are in any way tractable as long as we operate with some inadequate philosophical psychology, one for instance that makes the mind a dwelling-place of elementary contents, or that lacks a properly developed analysis of observer's (i.e. behavioural) psychology, or that quite ignores the subtle twists of the concept of mental directedness or 'intentionality' which we owe to Brentano, Meinong and Husserl.

The second important matter which comes up for philosophical consideration is the claim of certain valuations to be mandatory, to be such as all who reflect enough *must* and *should* accept, and *must* and *should* apply to everyone and exact from everyone. The 'must' of sheer necessity here appears in a close marriage with a peculiar case of 'shouldness' or normativity, which to many philosophers seems the height of confusion, but which none the less always comes back in what we feel deeply disposed to say. How shall we deal with such mandatoriness? Is it merely a descriptive character of certain valuations that they thus arrogate authority to themselves, without being able to exclude a counter-arrogation of authority by contrary valuations? Or are there ways in which we can test, and by testing validate or invalidate, the authority claimed by such mandatory valuations? And if there are none such, is the whole uttering of mandatory valuations not vain and unprofitable, since finding them means no more than adopting them, and adopting them has no necessary influence on others? Or does mandatoriness involve the real presence in objects and states of affairs of obscure predicates and modalities which in non-mandatory valuations only *appear* to be present? If so, we have not merely the problem of the tests for such 'real presence', but the further problem as to why such real presence is connected with emotion or endeavour in ourselves, a connection not met with in other cases of cognition. But perhaps mandatoriness consists rather in some built-in self-restriction to what could be pursued or chosen by anyone for anyone, and perhaps such an austere notion will enable us in some way to 'deduce' the rich variety of what we ordinarily take to be mandatory values. That such a view can be sustained will be argued for in the last chapter of the present monograph. For the time being we may argue that while the concept of mandatory valuation involves profound difficulties, these need not lead to that discrediting of it as a concept that has been frequent in recent times: it should rather lead to the discrediting of the assumptions, by no means perspicuous, which have made it seem discreditable. There is nothing self-evident in the opinion that our emotions are in all cases only variable, personal reactions with nothing but a contingent relation to that which calls them forth, or to that on which they are directed: innumerable linguistic and conceptual facts belie such a simple-minded theory. The elenchus of Moore may in any case be applied to all valid mandatory valuations: we may say that we know that there are some such, and that we have much more certainty regarding them, than we have in regard to any psychological or semantic or ontological theory which would conjure them out of existence.

From questions regarding the possibility of mandatory valuations, we pass on to questions concerned with the overall structure of mandatory values and disvalues, to what we shall call in later chapters the construction of a 'value-firmament'. If mandatory values represent merely a piece of would-be legislation for all in regard to all, such questions of overall structure will at best systematise the values and disvalues of a single arrogant individual or society, but if the possibility of a validation is not merely claimed, but involved in the structure of such valuations, then we may hope to construct a firmament of values and disvalues which will be more than a mere product of personal pontification. Highly arguable firmaments of values may be held to be found in the axiologies of Scheler and Hartmann, as also of Moore,

Rashdall and Ross. We are at least here in the presence of in-finitely discussable issues, and not among the mere Babel of conflicting voices which on certain conceptions of valuation would be all that was to be expected. Plainly the penetration to valid mandatory values is in some manner really possible: the only legitimate task for philosophy is to discover *how* this is the case.

The mapping of a firmament of values, and the consideration of the relations among them, must lead on to a further question: the relation of mandatory values to purely personal values, of the relation of sorts of things that everyone must value for everyone, to the sorts of things that each individual only values for himself. We have here the choices of trying to make the two classes of values wholly independent, or of giving them an essential bearing upon each other, the mandatory values being, for instance, essentially regarded as values of higher order, which are built upon and presuppose the existence of purely personal values which they only order and systematise. This latter is essentially the conception of Butler who sees the higher faculties of self-love and benevolence, and at a further remove conscience, as ordering the particular passions, and as having no possible content without the latter, whereas the former is the view suggested by certain intemperate passages in Kant where it would seem that a total lack of non-mandatory impulses would be of advantage to pure members of the Kingdom of Ends.

And our mapping must lead on finally to a discussion like that in the fifth chapter of Moore's *Principia Ethica* as to the relation of our value-map to conduct, or like many of those that occur in Ross's *Right and the Good* or *The Foundations of Ethics*. Are values and disvalues, mandatory or personal, sufficient to decide what we should do in a given situation, or shall we hold that there are practical principles which go beyond them, and which are not formulable in terms of them? And do values and disvalues decide what we ought to do in some simple, general manner, perhaps involving a general metric of values and disvalues, or are the principles that enable us to reach practical decision many and complex? Are there perhaps practical principles, unconditional 'oughts' for conduct, to which all considerations of value and disvalue are irrelevant? Is it further the case that purely personal factors enter into our practical decisions, and that they *should* be allowed to supplement and to give a definite outcome to our practical problems. These questions have also been considered by the philosophers we are to study, though we may be somewhat critical of some of their opinions.

We have said enough to indicate the range of concepts and problems covered by axiological ethics. Let us now consider the views actually put forward by our chosen exponents.

II. BRENTANO AND MEINONG

The present chapter will deal with the contributions to axiology and axiological ethics of Franz Brentano (1838–1917) and Alexius Meinong (1853–1920), both of whom illuminated valuation and value by placing it in the context of a truly profound, magnificently elaborated philosophy of mind. The work of both philosophers, like that of Christian von Ehrenfels, another value-theorist of the period (*System der Werttheorie – System of Value-Theory* – 1897–8), is associated with Austria: Brentano's most brilliant period of teaching was in Vienna, Meinong created and operated a small philosophical school at Graz, while von Ehrenfels taught for many years at Prague. There is something characteristically Austrian about all their work, a neat accuracy together with a fighting shy of the murky enthusiasm and the ill-justified comprehensiveness of the typical Germanic 'system'.

Brentano, with whom we shall first deal, was of course primarily a philosophical psychologist, the developer of a 'psychognosy', an analysis of mentality as such and its basic differentiations, whose empirical connections he was concerned to stress, though it seems to a modern student a severely conceptual study. This philosophical psychology was expounded in the *Psychologie vom empirischen Standpunkte* (*Psychology from the Empirical Standpoint*) of 1878 (second augmented edition in 1910), and provided the foundation of an axiological ethics, first expounded in a famous lecture entitled *The Origin of our Knowledge of Right and Wrong* (*Vom Ursprung sittlicher Erkenntnis*, 1889) and whose further development can be studied in the posthumously published *Grundlegung und Aufbau der Ethik* (*Foundations and Structure of Ethics*). The lecture on the *Origin of our Knowledge of Right and Wrong* was translated into English by Cecil Hague in 1902, and Moore wrote of it in 1903 in the *International Journal of Ethics*, vol. XIV; 'This is a far better discussion of the most fundamental

16

principles of Ethics than any others with which I am acquainted. . . . In almost all points in which he differs from any of the great historical systems, he is in the right. It would be difficult to exaggerate the importance of this work.' This great lecture, thus endorsed by a great philosopher, has long been out of print in England, but we are glad to see it retranslated in 1969 by Roderick Chisholm.

Brentano's psychognosy may be roughly sketched for the purposes of the present monograph. Its great originality lay in a subtle modification of the scholastic notion of 'intention', the form *in* the mind which enables the mind to refer to what is not part of itself, and to what may or may not exist in the real world beyond itself. Only while the scholastic 'intention' was a strange piece of machinery designed to carry out a strange task, on which it threw not the smallest light, Brentano substituted the task for the machinery, the performance for the instrument, so that an intention ceased to be something that *explained* mental transcendence, and simply became a case of transcendence itself. In this self-transcendence, this intentionality of the mental, Brentano refused to see anything queer or requiring explanation: mentality is simply a plane where life is lived outside of itself, points beyond itself, is concerned with matters 'objective' to itself, and which need not, though they also may, be part and parcel of their own make-up or structure. This magnificent turning of a difficulty into a concept, and a problem into an explanation, is one of the most astonishing, because also most simple, philosophical feats: it simply consists in recognising what is most deeply characteristic of 'consciousness' and the life of mind. Psychic phenomena, acts of mind, can never be fully described in terms of their mere characters or elements or internal structure, but only also in terms of what they intend (and of how they intend it), of what they are directed to, of what in a non-linguistic sense they 'mean'.

Brentano of course was concerned to use his notion of self-transcendence in order to demarcate the realm of 'psychic or mental phenomena' from those that are 'physical', and it is perhaps doubtful whether he achieved this. But whether or not there are non-intentional states of mind, or cases of intentionality which are not mental, the notion remains of supreme importance in illuminating the higher levels of mental life, on which such performances as valuations can take place. And experienced intentionality has an importance which non-experienced intentionality (if the notion is at all legitimate) never can achieve. If animal behaviour or neural states have their own peculiar directedness to transcendent matters of concern, we can know of such directedness only through indirect, never quite reliable indices, whereas experienced intentionality has its own directly experienced directedness. We cannot in fact know that we are minding anything without knowing what we are minding. Brentano's theory of intentionality of course includes a further Aristotelian view of the way in which intentionality, while primarily directed outwards, to what is *not* part of itself, also embraces a subsidiary direction to itself, so that the intention towards X is also subsidiarily an intention to this intention, a doctrine that does not (according to Brentano) lead to an infinite regress owing to the manner in which such subsidiary, self-directed intentionality melts into and blends with its primary, outward-turned basis. And it sets in an emphatic light a point previously stressed by Aristotle and the Schoolmen: that the directedness of mind, not being a relation, does not demand the existence or being of what it intends. Its object enters into its inner description without entering it as a real part, and without needing to be a real part of anything anywhere.

The relevance of Brentano's doctrine to value-theory lies, however, not in his general demarcation of the mental, but in his peculiar classification of mental phenomena. Following Descartes, for whose insights he has a profound respect, he believes in *three* fundamental forms of experienced self-transcendence, one of which is the most simple and basic of all, the second of which is built upon and presupposes the first, while the last is built upon the second and hence indirectly on the first. The first is the *Vorstellung*, the simple Presentation or presence of something to consciousness, without any further stance towards such an object being taken up by the mind. Such presentations may be sensuous, they may also be purely cogitative, and they may be of physical things or states of things, real or imaginary, and also of psychical acts directed upon such things or upon other psychical acts. Imposed on the *Vorstellung* is the act of Belief or Judgement, characterised by a unique antithesis between acceptance and rejection. Such beliefs or judgements are for Brentano the true existential or reality-experiences: in them an object or content comes before us, not merely as being this or that, but as being truly there or not there, or as being the case or not being the case. Brentano deprecates all analyses which place the essence of judging in an association of concepts: this is a pure matter of the *Vorstellung*, of unconvinced presentation. Imposed on Judgement and *Vorstellung* alike we then have the 'Phenomena of Love and Hate', characterised by quite another kind of acceptance and rejection than that of the Judgement: they are cases in which some object is positively embraced as good (though the word 'good' may of course not be available) or rejected as bad. Brentano believes that this unique sort of acceptance and rejection, as unanalysable as that of Belief, runs through states of feeling, states of desire, and states of will alike, and this whether they are warm and excited or calm and cool. Distant approval and warm espousal (or their contraries) have precisely the same note of acceptance (or rejection), and so have the most inchoate wish and the most firmly adopted resolution. In all these cases we are, as it were, saying *Placet* or *Fiat* or their contraries, with what further overtones is a matter of basic unimportance. Plainly there is a deep introspective warrant for the affinity here noted by Brentano. The close relation of conative–affective acceptance–rejection to the acceptance–rejection of Judgement, comes out in the systematic variation of the form of Love and Hate with that of Belief: whether an attitude is one of Hope, Fear, Desire, Vague Wish or Firm Resolve, Action or mere Satisfaction or Dissatisfaction depends throughout on what we *believe* to be the case. Plainly we are dealing with axiomatic principles: it is not, for example, meaningful to resolve upon the plainly impossible or to be satisfied with what is seen not to be the case. Brentano further illuminates his concept of affective–

conative acceptance–rejection by affirming the unanalysable character of *preference*. Preference does not consist in any relation of superior strength or intensity among our variously directed wants or likes – an error committed in many discussions of voluntary freedom – but in the unique stance of liking or wanting one thing *above* or *rather than* another. (Much as the partial beliefs studied in probability-theory are simple stances rather than embroiled belief-tendencies.) Plainly there is a kind of preference which conforms to the conflict-of-strength pattern, and Brentano has no wish to deny it, but he is utterly right in recognising that truly interesting form of preference (of which choice is the supreme expression) which is unitary rather than divided.

Brentano's theory now takes a new turn, of great importance for the theory of valuation. He believes that the experiences of Belief or Judgement, in which the reality of what we believe seems to flood in upon us, have a limiting form in which it no longer makes sense to question the authenticity of what one judges to be there: its reality is itself present to us. Brentano following Descartes believes in a clear and distinct perception which it does not make sense to doubt: the fact, the true posture of things, is then *evident* to us. If this Evidence (*Evidenz*) of Brentano is interpreted as a sort of inner feeling contingently related to the content present, the theory is of course worthless: no experience, in the sense of mere inner feeling, if such there can be, can amount to the evident truth or reality of anything. But it must be remembered that Brentanos 'experiences' are not the experiences of the empiricists and the phenomenalists, merely states of being thus and thus subjectively. They are essentially transcendences, states of living beyond self, and it is arguable that transcendences which fall short of their mark, or which *may* fall short of their mark, all presuppose a limiting transcendence in which what is the case simply declares itself, so that only a false philosophy of mind can make what is thus declared seem doubtful. Brentano follows Descartes in making such cases of evident self-declaration rare. He confines them to our assurance of the existence and certain characters of our own inner attitudes, and of the truth of certain simple axioms. He does not, like Meinong, spread the net of a probabilistic self-evidence rather wide, nor like Moore maintain that we *know* many things that it would not be self-contradictory to deny.

The theory of a limiting, self-declaratory truth in the realm of Belief leads, however, to a parallel doctrine in the realm of Love and Hate and Preference. There are some cases of liking or disliking or preferring which are characterised (*charakterisiert*) by an inner rightness (*Richtigkeit*) which it is as senseless to try to circumvent or ignore as it would be to do so in the case of the inner clinch of self-evidence. These axiological clinches have not to do with the reality of things, but with the worthiness or appropriateness of our own attitudes to them or vice versa: we can as little evade (though we may of course refuse to be deflected by) the peculiar pressure of a worthy love or hate or preference, as we can evade the quite different pressure of what shows itself as evident, as being plainly the case.

Brentano's view of the precise character of this inner correctness of acts of love, hate and preference, is, however, obscure: he says that certain acts are characterised by such inner correctness, but it is not clear how such 'characterising' is to be interpreted. It might mean that *we* characterise such acts as correct in a judgement which will, of course, have to have the highest self-evidence. On such a view it will be this *judgement*, rather than the loving and hating as such, which will mediate correctness for us. Of such a view, which Meinong afterwards espoused, there is no clear trace in Brentano: it is of the essence of his theory that it is in loving and hating correctly that the good or bad is brought home to us, not by judging as to the correctness of our loving and hating: the good and bad are simply the objects of correct love and hate. What then does 'being characterised as correct' entail if it does not entail an extrinsic judgement? Two answers are possible: it may merely mean that certain acts of loving and hating *are* correct, have correctness as a *property*, though they need not, and perhaps could not meaningfully, be *experienced* as correct, or it may mean that they not only *are* correct, but are in some sense *experienced*, or capable of being experienced, as correct. If the former is assumed, some sort of a judgement or presentation will be necessary to bring this correctness into our ken, and we shall be back in our previous position. The latter is therefore what Brentano must mean, and Chisholm is therefore faithful to Brentano's intention, if not to his German, in translating the phrase 'als richtig charakterisiert' as 'experienced as correct'. Here, however, many will object that while we can intend correctness, we cannot in any sense live through it, have it as part of our lived experience. We here require a ruling as to the most suitable and in a sense true use of the verb 'to experience', and we shall here accept the view that there are and can be characters which can be thought of, intended, but which can also be livingly part of our experience, of our intimate selves, even when we do not intend them. Thus we can *experience* succession as well as project it and perceive it, and we can experience such features of succession as smooth continuity, sharp change, fragmentation into brief phases, etc. In the same way we can live through passivity and live through activity: our experiences *qua* experiences have passivity or activity as internal characters. It is arguable likewise, *pace* Hume, that we often experience our own identity in the sense of a selfsameness to which varied things happen. If all these cases of experiencing are possible, then there seems no good reason why we should not experience correctness, and there is certainly a sense of inner authority in many of our more considered valuations. But the trouble is now that if correctness can be thus experienced, we cannot be wrong about it: an act of love or hate, experienced as correct, simply is, as an experience, correct. Here we obviously require some doctrine of a simulacrum of correctness which in the limiting case fades into correctness itself, a doctrine that many would reject as absurd, but which to others would seem to have the obvious stamp of truth. Correctness and evident truth are the standards both of themselves and their contraries, and while Duessa may succeed in her deceits in the absence of Fidessa, she cannot sustain them in Fidessa's presence. God conceived as the last stronghold of the evidently correct plainly cannot require an infinite certification of His correctness. But as Brentano has not considered these questions, we shall not debate them further.

Brentano, however, buttresses his doctrine by a series of concrete examples, which are not less valuable on account of their entire obviousness. The first is that of our love for clear insight into things, and our hatred of error and ignorance. We not only feel impelled to have the attitudes in question: we also feel them to be appropriate, correct. What Brentano holds will of course arouse immense dissent: it will be pointed out that we often wish to remain ignorant of something, that some find all knowledge profitless and senseless, etc. The point of the example remains: to say that we do not care for knowledge, that we prefer error, always requires special explanation. It is in itself a perverse utterance, which requires special circumstances to justify it, whereas the contrary valuation simply make good sense, is undistorted, standard, normative. All consciousness, all speech, has a basic interest in fact and truth which only the mutely unconscious (if they could repudiate anything) could with full sense repudiate. What is here plain is even more plain in Brentano's next case: joy and sadness. To like sadness and shrink from joy, is a perfectly possible, not infrequently realised state of mind, but it involves what can only be called a perverse liking of one's own dislikes and their objects, and a perverse dislike of one's own likings and their objects. Brentano's third example is that of a love of rightness in our own attitudes of love and hate: there is something deeply perverse, though of course entirely possible, in loving to be incorrect. Other examples, seemingly tautological but not truly so, are the rightness of preferring a good, i.e. an object of correct love, to an evil, an object of correct hatred, or the existence of a good to its non-existence, or the non-existence of an evil to its existence, or a sum of several goods to only one among them, or an intense degree of something good to a weaker form of the same, etc. These apparently trivial examples are the truly basic ones, rather than such loaded instances as the evil of incest, a complex matter on which, even if the case were objectively clear, no one could possibly have a reliable experience or insight. Brentano admits that he cannot feel the correctness or incorrectness of preferring high-minded love to intellectual insight or vice versa, he even considers that it would be a reasonable inference from this lack of experience that there is *no* correctness or incorrectness in the matter. (See *Origin*, §§ 31, 32.)

We shall not here attempt to enter into the detailed pronouncements of Brentano's posthumously published *Foundations and Structure of Ethics*. It discusses most questions regarding right and wrong, good and evil, the freedom of the will, etc., that moral philosophers have discussed, including some that the scholastics discussed but which have dropped out of the straitened ethical discussions of modern times. Since Brentano believes in ethical *knowledge*, even if such knowledge is a built-in feature of our emotional and practical attitudes, he also has a place for ethical probability, and can discuss the views of the probabilists and the tutiorists, the rigorists and the laxists, moral tribes which exist now as in the middle ages, but which somehow elude the notice of moral philosophers. The main defect of Brentano is obvious: he has presented us with too many unanalysed ultimates and too many unjustified intuitions. One has a strong feeling that he has really unearthed the true foundations both of the mind and the realm of value, but one also feels that his intuitions are not enough, that one requires more clarity in his basic conceptions (e.g. correctness) and more justification for his remarkable insights. Otherwise we have nothing with which to counter Sade or Nietzsche or one or other of the dark mentors whose shrines have been recently refurbished.

If we now turn to Meinong, we have what is probably the most brilliantly elaborated of all theories of the possibility of what may be called 'emotional knowledge', and an interesting application of this theory to many of the main formal questions concerning value and disvalue, merit and demerit, rightness and wrongness· His main writings on axiology are all to be found in the recently published third volume of the new Collected Edition of his works. These are: *Psychologisch-ethische Untersuchungen zur Werththeorie* (*Psychological-Ethical Investigations into Value-Theory*) (1894), *Über emotionale Präsentation* (*On Emotional Presentation*) (1917), *Zur Grundlegung der allgemeinen Werttheorie* (*Foundations of General Value-Theory*) (1923) and *Ethische Bausteine* (*Ethical Building-Stones*) (first published in 1969). As our aim is not to set forth the history of his opinions, we shall study them in their latest stage of development, with a rearward glance at some of the earlier treatments.

Meinong builds his value-theory on the intentionalist doctrine of Brentano: that it is of the essence of mental life to live outside of itself, to point beyond itself, and to concern itself with objects that need not be part of it, and which need not have being any-where, though, of course, they may be essential elements of reality, and known as such. The intentionalist psychology of Brentano was, however, elaborated and complicated in a large number of ways, not all of which matter from the point of view of value-theory, and some not from any point of view. Meinong introduces the novel concept of the *Annahme* or Assumption, a mental attitude which has most of the characters of the judge-ment, and may even imitate the conviction of the judgement, without involving any genuine conviction, without making a committed reference to what really is the case. This *Annahme* or Assumption takes the place of the *Vorstellung* or Presentation in the psychology of Brentano, the latter being treated as a merely sensational experience in which we live through contents which may indeed offer material for a Judgement or Assumption, but which do not of themselves truly present objects. The main point of the new doctrine is to make the mere entertainment of some possibility a *defective mode* of objective reference, rather than a basic mode upon which a Judgement is then built. The doctrine is interesting but not germane to our purpose: in practice there is little difference between the unconvinced contemplative assumption of Meinong and the Presentation of Brentano, except that the former expresses itself in a propositional rather than a 'thing'-directed form.

Meinong also has difficulty in accepting Brentano's belief in one psychic ground-class of Loving and Hating underlying all conative and affective phenomena: he harks back to the old dualism of Feeling and Desire, which he feels has a firm basis in introspection. But since, in his theory of valuation, he comes to admit that valuation rests jointly on both sorts of experience, he in effect admits that feeling and desire are, as it were, two modes of a single basic attitude, which is simply the point made by Brentano. Meinong therefore ends with a basic triplicity not very far from Brentano's three ground-classes of mental intention: a triplicity of unconvinced contemplation, of convinced judgement and of the affective-desiderative side of human life. And while Meinong has a more complex theory of the presupposition of the lower types of intention by the higher, he holds a similar view of the presupposition by feelings and desires of the acts of belief and contemplation which, as it were, offer them an objective material, and condition their form. Whether one desires X or is satisfied by X depends, for example, on whether one believes X to be the case or not: one cannot desire what one believes to be already realised nor be satisfied with what one believes to be unrealised. There are, however, acts of feigned belief or disbelief which make it possible for me to be as-it-were-satisfied by what I know to be unreal, or as-it-were-desirous of what I know to be the case, so that these presuppositional conditions are less restrictive than would at first seem to be the case.

Meinong, however, departs from Brentano in two fundamental respects, both important for value-theory. He teaches a new doctrine of mental 'contents', borrowed from the Polish philosopher Twardowski, which as it were reinstates the scholastic doctrine of the intention '*in* the mind' by which reference 'beyond the mind' is made possible. He also attempts an indefinite widening of the concepts of *object* to which intentional reference is possible. As regards the former of these innovations, Meinong holds that intentionality is always two-sided: it has, we may say, its me-wardness and its object-wardness, its relation to my subjective mindedness or *Zumutesein*, on the one hand, and its relation to objects of varying sorts, on the other. It is, moreover, only by having a specific me-wardness or immanent *content*, that it can have a specific object-wardness or transcendent objectivity. (The terms 'me-wardness' and 'object-wardness' are not Meinongian, but are used for elucidatory purposes.) This two-sidedness occurs even in so simple a case as that of sense-givenness, the hearing of a note, the seeing of a colour, etc. In such an experience we can distinguish the objective datum that comes before us and is given to us, e.g. the loud, high note or the bright, oblong, red patch, etc., and the specific manner in which our own experience is modified to make such a presentation possible, a manner that we can in the cases in question perhaps call a loudwise, highwise manner, or an oblongwise, brightwise, redwise manner. (The use of the termination -wise to express contents is convenient but not Meinongian.) We are otherwise minded according as we mind this or that sort of thing or state of things: there are as many nuances of immanent subjectivity as there are nuances of transcendent objectivity, and there is an absolute, necessary correlation, despite unbridgeable difference, between the one and the other. Each subjective content is the appointed medium through which an objective feature is brought home to the experiencing mind. The manner in which the painful rending of our flesh makes us aware of the sharpness of the instrument that rends it may serve as an analogy – though only as an analogy – of the essential two-sidedness which Meinong sees in all genuine conscious reference. (Except in such as is purely a symbolic substitute for the true seeing or thinking of something.)

Meinong's doctrine has been thought unplausible by many. Thus Moore in an Aristotelian Society paper of 1909–10 denied that he could detect a subjective *Zumutesein* in sensation which corresponded to, but which was not identical with, the sense-datum of which he was conscious, and the writings of Wittgenstein are full of eloquent denials that there is anything common to all the experiences in which we consider this or that feature of objects. On the other hand, the very fact that philosophers have been as ready to adopt sensation- as sense-datum language regarding sense-given qualities bears testimony to the two-sidedness Meinong believes in: we can for example, experience brightness, loudness, etc., as specific impacts on ourselves, or as characters given 'out there' in things. And there is abundant testimony, e.g. in Bradley, Wittgenstein and others, as to how the objective content of the most complex intellectual references can collapse, as it were, into a mere nuance of interior experience to which no better word than 'feeling' seems apposite. If all this is true, then all conscious references as are more than the mere readiness to use symbols appropriately – which is of course all that conscious references ever are for certain philosophers – can be condensed into nuances of interior feeling, but from this it also follows that such nuances of personal feeling are capable of a 'projection', an exteriorisation, in virtue of which they may set before us certain non-identical but necessarily correlated features of objects. The subjective variations of our personal conviction may, for example, set before us the probabilities, the likelihoods, that seem part and parcel of the perceived world. And this leaves open the yet more interesting possibility that the valuations which have their me–wardness in subjective feeling, may have a correlated, objective aspect which is, at least in some cases, a transcendent feature of the world.

Meinong further departs from Brentano, who has an Aristotelian faith in the prime reality of individual things, in believing that there are many different types of *object* which can be set up for us by differing types of intentional experience. Not only can we deal with objects of lowest order, the *things* of ordinary diction or their simple parts and aspects: we can also put before ourselves objects of higher order, such as the way first-order objects are *related* to other objects, and the complex *patterns* they thereby form, and also the *states of affairs* (called by Meinong 'objectives') which concern first-order (and also higher-order) objects, such as that this is to the left of that, this is larger than that, there is this or that actually in existence, if this were a so-and-so it would also be a such-and-such and so on. The notion of the circumstance or state of affairs as a unique kind of object of conscious reference was anticipated by the Stoic doctrine of λεκτά and by Bolzano's doctrine of Propositions-in-themselves (*Sätze an sich*), but it was Meinong who first gave them a prominent place in philosophy, coining for them the strange name of 'objective'.

From the recognition of objects treated in the incompleteness they have for our thought, there was a natural passage to the recognition of objects that have no being at all, the round square which does not and cannot exist, or the equality of Paris to London in size, which is not the case though it can be entertained in thought. It is highly arguable that human experience, even at the level of perception, is rich in objects that go beyond the concrete existent things of an individualist ontology: the world around us seems full of bearings, of suggestions, of half-formed possibilities, of pin-pointed facts or circumstances, of gaps, of vaguenesses, of generalities, of unrealized limits, and it is a matter of dogma rather than direct experience that all these higher-order things will reduce to individuals and their actual properties. It is this recognition of higher-order objectivity of various sorts which characterises Meinong's theory of objects, and which leaves a place for the values which are so unquestionably part of the ordinary look of the world, pervading things and also floating above them as standards or norms, until they are banished from the picture by the limited aims of science and the prejudices of a scientific philosophy.

Meinong of course went further than most thinkers could readily approve in giving to all his classes of objects not merely a status as objects of thought, but even a status independent of thought and mental reference. It is well known and notorious that Meinong argued that even non-existent and absurd objects needed to be *something* in order to be absent from the universe, in order to be excluded by the actual state of things. This notorious opinion is, however, neither as absurd nor as ill worked out as it is commonly thought to be, nor are the well-known attempts of Russell and others to take the legs from under it or to find substitutes for it, as successful as they are commonly thought to have been. It is not, however, necessary for our purposes to argue for the ontological position of all Meinong's higher-order entities: it is sufficient to say that they can be and often are genuine objects of our perceptual and thought-intentions as much as the individual things that are by many alone supposed to be real, and that our attitudes of valuation are as much directed to *them* as to any concrete thing that exists in the world. A mind that cannot pin-point circumstances and direct attitudes to them specifically, or that cannot see things in one-sided incompleteness as well as in concrete completeness, or that cannot treat the non-existent and even the absurd as if it were actual, is not a mind that can fully savour the values and excellences of things. The whole value of logic, for instance, is derived from a contrast with the absurd. Language enables us to perform all these feats with precision, but they are often performed less precisely at the level of unformulated perception, action and feeling.

We must, however, turn to the precise theory of valuation which Meinong fitted into his philosophy of mind, and the precise theory of values which he added to his theory of objects. On Meinong's view, valuation is primarily a matter of feeling, and only secondarily and derivatively a matter of desire. The principal reason he gives for this view is the somewhat inconclusive one that it is not because we desire (or are averse from) objects or states of affairs that we have feelings towards them, but because we have feelings towards them that we have positive or negative desires for them. Such feelings do not demand that their objects actually exist or are present, but only that they are imagined, assumed to be there. Valuation is, however, feeling (and secondarily desire) which presupposes *judgement*, rather than mere contemplative presentation, and which is, moreover, wrought up with the *content* (in Meinong's technical sense of 'content') of such judgement. In other words, when we value things, we are concerned with their *existence* or *non-existence*, their *real being* or *non-being* in the world, and we are concerned with the real being or non-being of the *specific sorts of objects* we have before us in thought, and which are set before us through the *content* of our experience. Valuation is, in other words, highly specific existence-love or existence-hatred: what we value, we want to *be* and do not want *not* to be, and are pleased to see *existing* and not to see *not existing*, and we want *it* specifically to be, and not some *other* object or sort of object.

The sense of this analysis will become plainer if we contrast valuation with other types of emotional or desirous attitude to objects. There is, Meinong says, such a thing as knowledge-love or hatred in which we indeed delight and enquire after what exists or is the case, and turn from what does not exist or is not the case, but which is not = valuation, since we do not care about the *specific content* of what exists or is the case (or does not exist or is not the case). Such an emotional-desiderative attitude is concerned with real being, and is therefore judgement-based, but it is not a case of valuation, since it is after existence and fact *whatever they may turn out to be*. It lacks a specific *bias* towards certain alternatives which is always present in valuation. Thus if I value fair dealing, I deplore its lack or its contrary, whereas a scientific student of society is as interested in an unfair as in a fair society. (Meinong does not confuse scientific interest with the valuation *of* knowledge as such: it is an interest in what is the case, not in *my* knowing it.) Valuation also stands opposed to emotional-desiderative attitudes which do not presuppose judgement, and are indifferent to the real, or to what is the case. Ordinary satisfaction and dissatisfaction are of this sort: our delight in a warm bath is unshaken by the scientific conviction that heat is merely a secondary quality. Our aesthetic satisfactions and dissatisfactions are also of this sort: questions of the reality or unreality of what aesthetically pleases or displeases us are quite irrelevant, and this is why we say we may be aesthetically pleased with something as an aesthetic spectacle or mere show whose reality would horrify us. But aesthetic satisfactions and dissatisfactions have the same close tie with *content* that valuations also have, and this differentiates them from ordinary satisfactions and dissatisfactions. The Meinongian theory of aesthetic appreciation was interestingly worked out by his pupil Stefan Witasek in his *Aesthetik*. Meinong does not speak of aesthetic valuation or aesthetic values nor of intellectual valuation or values: the aesthetic and purely scientific lack the concern with the *precise content of reality* which is characteristic of valuation and values. Meinong's analyses may seem arid and arbitrary, but have arguably lighted on a central point which other analyses of valuation often pass over. It is not merely delighting in something or urgently wanting it for ourselves, which constitutes valuation, but considering it as a contribution to the total real universe and delighting in it or wanting it in such a context. Moore plainly agrees with Meinong: he too discovers the goodness or badness of things by considering them either as being all there is, or as contributing to wider totals of existence.

It may here be noted that Meinong regards our attitude to an object's *non*-existence as having an equal importance in valuation with our attitude to its existence: if we value things we feel positively towards their existence and negatively towards their non-existence, and if we value things negatively we feel positively towards their non-existence and negatively towards their existence. But he also notes that the strength of these components is not normally equal: there are some things which we value mainly in so far as we would *miss* them if absent, without taking much positive delight in their presence, whereas there are other things which we value mainly in so far as we delight in their presence but perhaps would not miss if absent. This distinction is afterwards to recur in Hartmann's concepts of the 'height' and 'strength' of value, and is also in harmony with Meinong's own classifications of the morally good, the correct, the permissible and the morally evil. But in his posthumous *Grundlegung* he adopts the unacceptable doctrine that it would be *rational* to be just as pleased or displeased with a thing's absence as we were displeased or pleased with its presence, and vice versa, a doctrine that entails that we ought always to be infinitely sorry for all the countless good things which do not exist, and infinitely glad for all the countless bad things which do not exist, resulting in a frame of feeling that is quite indeterminate. This doctrine is a mistake in an otherwise fine analysis.

Meinong now makes use of his doctrine of 'content' to give an objective meaning to values and similar predicates. If *all* our objective references intend features of objects by a peculiar *use* (which need not be construed as at all like a causal inference) of modifications of inner feeling (in a very wide sense of the word 'feeling'), then the modifications of feeling in the ordinary, narrow sense of the word may also be used to mediate objective references, may serve to introduce us to properties perhaps transcendently 'out there' in things. If we can be made aware of extension and shape in things by being made to feel a correlative, but unbridgeably different, drawn-outness and patterning of our interior sensibility, then the pleasure, displeasure and desire with which we are affected may also serve to introduce us to suitabilities, unsuitabilities or requirements, real or imaginary, which are seen, not in ourselves, but in things. The mystery and difficulty of the use of what is 'internal' to bring before us what is 'external' is no greater in one case than the other: it is in fact, properly regarded, no difficulty at all. Meinong writes:

> That we are here dealing with more than mere possibilities is shown by a group of entirely everyday attributions such as those we encounter when someone speaks of a pleasant bath, fresh air, oppressive heat, vexatious noise, beautiful colour, a gay or sad, tedious or entertaining story, a sublime work of art, excellent people, good intentions, etc. The close relations of such attributes to our feelings is not open to question, but it is just as unquestionable that they are, as attributes, completely analogous to the other properties set before us by presentative ideas in quite familiar fashion. If I say of the sky that it is blue, and again say of it that it is beautiful, I seem to credit the sky with a property in one case as in the other, and since a feeling participates in the apprehension of the relevant property in the one case while an idea does the work in the other it is natural to ascribe the presentative function to the feeling in the former case as we do to an idea in the latter (*On Emotional Presentation*, p. 33)

Meinong goes on to distinguish and name the peculiar objective features which we apprehend through our feelings and desires: he calls them *dignitatives* in the case of our feelings, and *desideratives* in the case of our desires. The basic dignitatives are four in number corresponding to the four basic types of emotional attitude: the agreeable (revealed by 'ordinary' feelings), the beautiful (revealed by aesthetic feelings), the authentically true (truth as a dignitative, revealed by 'knowledge–feelings') and the good or valuable (revealed by existence–feelings). The desideratives are various types of 'ought' (*Sollen*), revealed by various types of desire. On Meinong's view, the objective world with which we have commerce is not only peopled with things and facts, but also with dignities and requirements, which latter we can only apprehend by being emotionally or desideratively moved. The purely detached intellect, which will not permit wants or feelings to colour the objective order of things, can never see that order as it completely and truly is: it can at most

33

see a reduced, incomplete world which is a reflex of its own heartlessness.

Meinong does not, however, espouse the view that *all* our feelings and desires reveal authentic dignities and requirements which are part of the structure of real being: only *some* of them do so. *Which* do so is, for Meinong, not a matter of wishful or emotive thinking: he is unwilling to accept Brentano's doctrine of an inwardly experienced rightness of certain acts of feeling or desire. Meinong thinks that an act of self-evident judgement, of *knowledge*, is here required: while our emotions and desires may people the world with dignities and requirements, it is a purely cognitive experience which determines which have an absolute status, which are there as part of the real structure of things. There is therefore a curious and elaborate mixture of the emotional and intellectual in Meinong's theory of true values and value-knowledge: emotions are necessary but not sufficient conditions of the latter. And, whether true or false, the theory is at least a *clear one*, not a mere muddle like the parallel accounts of Scheler and Hartmann which we shall study later. Only Richard Price, with his doctrine of a necessary tie-up between a perception of values by the understanding and a resultant affection of the heart, which that perception of necessity provokes, provides an alternative to Meinong's theory. But for Price emotion is a necessary consequence of value-perception, whereas for Meinong it is a necessary pre-condition.

If we, however, ask about the values concerning which Meinong believes himself to have firm knowledge, we shall not find that they are many: he is not like Moore, who claims clear intuitions regarding very many values. Meinong appeals vaguely to our appraisal of certain acts of military heroism and to the aesthetic dignity of certain Greek statues and German poems and musical compositions. He even suggests that the sort of self-evidence here at work is one for rational surmise rather than for uncontrovertible certainty, and that we may very well, in such a case, attach value to the judgements of *others*, and to the judgements of large numbers of reflective people.

The best example of value-insight in Meinong is, however, to be found in the careful analyses of moral value and duty which we have in the early *Psychological-Ethical Investigations into Value-Theory* of 1894, analyses which he was attempting to reformulate and modernize in the posthumously published *Ethical Building-Stones* (1969). Here Meinong distinguishes judgements of 'oughtness' from judgements of moral value, in that the former consider only the value of isolated acts, whereas the latter consider the values of permanent dispositions behind the acts. Meinong works out the logical relations of four classes of acts, the positively good, the correct, the allowable and the evil. Correct acts cover a small spectrum and pass over into positively good acts which are capable of indefinite degrees of goodness: allowable acts, likewise, cover a small spectrum and shade over into bad acts which are likewise capable of indefinite degrees. The omission of a positively good act is allowable, of a correct act positively bad, whereas the omission of an allowable act is positively good, and the omission of a bad act merely correct. Meinong further determines the goodness or badness of acts in terms of the extent to which altruism, regard for others, triumphs over self-interest. To be willing to make large sacrifices of self-interest for relatively small benefits to others has, for example, high positive goodness, provided it does not 'go to far', whereas moral evil is shown in the relatively large sacrifice of advantage to others for only a small advantage to oneself, or, more saliently, in the largeness of the personal sacrifice one is prepared to make for even a relatively small damage to others. Many axiomatic formulae are put forward and, whether or not they are quite acceptable, they at least show that the whole sphere of moral valuation has an inherent logic, and that it is infinitely far from the wholly vague pattern of emotional suasion and excuse which is alone recognised in certain modern treatments of ethical argument.

We may conclude this chapter with a brief mention of the value-system of von Ehrenfels, as expressed in *System der Werttheorie* (1897–8) in which desire, rather than feeling, serves as the primary value-fundamental, in which there is an application of the economic notion of marginal utility to the field of ethics – the *Grenzfrommen* is set beside the *Grenznutzen* – and in which there is also an interesting theory of value-movement, values being held to have an inherent tendency to move 'upwards' from nearer to remoter ends, 'downwards' from ends to means, 'inwards' from objects to attitudes towards objects, and also towards *activities* of a general sort from particular objects of such activities. This theory of value-movement is extremely important, in that it highlights the sort of non-rigorous logic which causes our values to change, and in that it disposes of any equation of rational, intersubjective values with unchangeable ones. It is plainly rational for values to change according to context, and among such contexts are for example, the over-production of certain values and the under-production of others. Only a moral philosopher would think that an act of extreme kindness or a spectacle of great beauty has the same value when seen in a Moravian mission-settlement, a German concentration camp, a club of heartless aesthetes, etc., or that there is no total field in which its value must be considered. It is clear, in conclusion, that 'axiology' owes a great deal to the Austrian school which started it off, and that the neglect into which that school's writings have fallen is deeply undeserved.

III. MOORE, RASHDALL AND ROSS

The present chapter will give some account of the development of axiological ethics in England. It is not possible to pass over the contributions of G. E. Moore, who, however much his discussions of the meaning of 'good', and his teachings concerning the 'naturalistic fallacy', may have made him the father of modern 'meta–ethics', was also one of the prime founders of axiology, concerned to construct an ordered map of the main 'heads' of value and disvalue, of the main sorts of things that are purely or admixedly good or bad. His contributions to this body of theory are mainly contained in the *Principia Ethica* of 1903; his later volume on *Ethics* (1912) and his various other writings on ethical and value-problems, including his very important 'Reply to my Critics' in the Schilpp volume on the *Philosophy of G. E. Moore*, do not discuss this kind of question to the same extent. Moore's drawing up of such a map of values in the last chapter of *Principia Ethica* is not only an important philosophical effort – *Principia Ethica* together with *Some Main Problems of Philosophy* and Russell's *Principles of Mathematics* are among the supreme products of British philosophising – it also set the tone for a most brilliant intellectual and aesthetic period, the true *belle époque* of Bloomsbury, which, with its odd mixture of subtle sophistication and naïve innocence, so much in key with the *Art Nouveau* and the Peace Palace and the other fantasies of the time, now appears, from the sad vista of our present debasements, as the last happy, lucid, hopeful breathing-space of civilised man. When Moore wrote that chapter men still believed in the possibility of the 'good life', and in the possibility of saying in what it might consist.

Moore begins his study of the Good, as is well known, with a long defence of the wholly unanalysable character of the notion of goodness, of goodness as such as opposed to being this or that sort of good thing. The philosophers of the past and present had been inclined to recommend this or that good thing – being pleased, being a source of pleasure, being what one desires to desire etc. – because they thought that such conditions were part and parcel of the notion of being good, so that it did not 'make sense' to suppose that there was a good state of affairs which did not fall under such a head. In so arguing, philosophers indeed gave their pronouncements a certain indubitability, but at the cost of making them trivial. For if all 'good' means is that one is pleased, or that things are as one desires to desire them, then the statement that being pleased is good or the only good, or that this is true of being as one desires to desire things to be, becomes a mere tautology, amounting to no more than saying that being pleased is being pleased, or that being as one desires to desire is being as one desires to desire. Yet those who make such statements do so often after much furrowing of brows and cogitative sweat: while taken, no doubt, to be necessary truths, they are also taken to be truths that represent an important step in thought. Being good is therefore as unanalysable as being yellow: it may stand in necessary relation to other last characters of things, just as being yellow stands to being one of the other colours, it may stand in various inductively established relations to other things as being yellow stands for certain frequencies of vibration; it may also be causally related to innumerable things which, as we say, are instrumentally good. But 'in itself' good remains a character that must be simply apprehended, that cannot be further analysed, and only when it has been thus apprehended, and clearly put before the mind in thought, can we come to understand and know various further propositions, necessary and empirical, concerning it.

Moore's opinion as to the unanalysable character of goodness seems to deprive it of all meaning, to transform it into a surd. For what can 'good' mean if it be cut off from all relations to feeling and practice, on the one hand, or from specific objects and sorts of object on the other? We seem back with the Megarians who denied the possibility of predicating anything of anything else, so that all one could say of unity was that it was unity and of goodness that it was goodness. And in a way we *are* brought back to the Megarians, since a view of predication which makes it consist in an external bond between contents isolable in thought *does* (*pace* Butler) destroy the meaning of predication. It is odd that 'yellow' should have been seen as the analogue of 'goodness', since being yellow is above all something that is only fully anything at all in the context of the full system of colours. It may be a logical error to make a whole a part of one of its parts, but it is not a logical error to make a relation to other constituent parts, and to some whole which they all form, a part of the *analysis*, the developed content of any and every part of certain whole systems. But whatever Moore's concessions to an exaggeratedly separative mode of conceiving or rather picturing things, in actual practice he makes the meaning of 'good' the centre of a large number of necessary, and countless probable connections, which are far more important elements in its meaning than the unanalysable nucleus on which he lays such emphasis. He believes, for example, that intuition or insight, a human experience, has some sort of profound connection with the presence of goodness in things – 'a certain unique predicate can be directly seen to belong' to this or that actual or possible existent (*Principia Ethica*, p. 60) – and he also believes that a special attitude of feeling and will is part of almost all cases where we think a thing good and all cases where we think so decidedly, and that 'a perception of goodness is probably included in the complex facts which we mean by willing and having certain kinds of feeling' (ibid., p. 131). He also presumes that 'good' means what is meant by 'ought to exist' (ibid., p. 17), thus giving it an intrinsic connection with existence, like Brentano and Meinong: in later treatments this relation to 'oughtness to exist' becomes 'synthetic' and not definitory. Moore also of course recognises that many concrete characters of things, e.g. being a state of affection, are bound up with being good and necessarily so.

Moore's doctrine of the naturalistic fallacy may therefore be regarded, not so much as a contribution to axiology, as to ontology or semantics, and, as a contribution to these latter, it follows the atomising, piecemeal sort of analysis favoured by traditional empiricism which must be acknowledged, after long experience, to be more productive of problems than of light. But in its relations to value-theory the doctrine of the naturalistic fallacy has had both good and bad results. It has, on the one hand, made us deeply aware of the wholly new dimension which springs into our ken when we value things instead of curiously and detachedly exploring them. It has, on the other hand, tended to make it appear that this new dimension has nothing whatever to do with 'the facts', with some sterilised sphere of pure science, a diremption which leads to many dogmatic simplifications. For it is arguable that the 'natures' of things, even as studied by science, are never without some relation to values and standards, which delimit what they are and what they can do, and that there can be no study of 'values in themselves' as divorced from necessary trends in certain segments of the conscious psyche, and perhaps even in unconscious and lifeless things.

If we now turn to Moore's concrete pronouncements on various axiological connections, we have, first of all, his somewhat sweeping, reductive analysis (afterwards mitigated) of what ought to be done. The assertion 'I am morally bound to perform this action' is held to be *identical* with the assertion 'This action will produce the greatest amount of good in the universe'. The reason for this extremely sweeping assertion is that only the greatest amount of value in the universe has the *uniqueness* necessary to the concept of duty: it could not be my duty to do any out of a large number of incompatible things (ibid., p. 147). This analysis of duty has, of course, the consequence that we can never be quite sure what our duty really is, since no one can follow out all the ramifying consequences of an act, and that there can be no certain rules of duty, only such as it is reasonable in the inherently doubtful circumstances to accept. The probabilism which is generally thought to be connected with casuistry is therefore connected with all practical ethics: practical ethics is essentially concerned with instrumental values, with what are the best means to a certain end, and in the estimation of such values questions of causal efficacy, always infinitely doubtful and inductive, necessarily enter. Moore's treatment is here very valuable, since he banishes what ought to be done from its central position in ethics, and recognizes the fact that, for all who reflect, it depends on a vast number of factors of which no sweeping account can be given.

It is, however, more than very doubtful whether Moore has given a good analysis, or even good characterisation, of what ought to be done. It is doubtful whether a strict 'ought' is a case of value at all, as it has many properties, e.g. its 'absoluteness' and lack of degree, which are not those of value. A deed that ought to be done is not necessarily a good deed, which means something more and different, and it is not even a deed that it is bad to omit, though this comes closer to the mark. Certainly, however, it has something intrinsic about it, and a certain imperative urgency, which is not explicable in terms of mere instrumentality. It is, further, extremely doubtful whether what ought to be done is ever to produce the greatest amount of good possible in the universe. Such an account assumes without argument that the bad can be weighed against the good, and it assumes without argument that the different kinds of good and bad can be weighed against one another, and it assumes, contrary to what we ordinarily hold, that it is our duty to produce the greatest possible addition of good for the universe, when the ordinary notion of duty plainly pledges us to much less, and has plainly a place for 'works of supererogation'. To depart so widely from ordinary notions plainly requires more argument than one based on the mere *uniqueness* of the notion in question.

The second interesting axiological contribution of Moore is his doctrine of Organic Wholes. While objects considered as what they are in themselves always and necessarily have the same value or disvalue, the wholes that they form may have values and disvalues which are in no sense the sum of, and not even plainly proportionate to, the values that enter into them. Thus pleasure, *per se* a thing of little worth, when associated with the awareness of what is worthy of admiration, *per se* also a thing of little worth, gives rise to the new whole of well-justified aesthetic pleasure which is one of the most valuable things in the universe. In the same way great pain, a very evil thing, associated with great wickedness, or choice of what is for other reasons evil, creates an evil which is decidedly less in amount than the evil of the pain plus the evil of the wickedness: wickedness requited, though it adds one evil to another, produces a result which mitigates both evils. Moore's principle is obviously fundamental in value-theory, but it is odd that it did not lead him to a related principle of context, which would have enabled him to make better sense of the 'organicism' of Hegel. Plainly a thing in a given context does *not* have the value or disvalue that it would have in isolation or in another context, and yet this contextual value or disvalue is *not* the same as the value of the whole in which it belongs. Thus a certain speech may be particularly gorgeous at a certain place in a tragedy, yet the tragedy need not therefore be particularly gorgeous and may, despite the speech, be a rather poor tragedy *on* the whole. Value *in* a whole is, in fact, not the same as value *on* the whole, and one would think the penetration of Moore would have reached down to this fact.

Moore further gives a rather interesting analysis of what he calls the beautiful, though he admits that it is not quite what is ordinarily meant by beauty, and is rather analogous to what Brentano meant by the 'good': the beautiful is what ought to be admired, or what, on the treatment of 'ought' Moore accepts, it is good to admire. Moore's definition of beauty enables him to explain why many unconscious natural objects, which he finds it hard to hold are *very* valuable apart from the aesthetic admiration they excite, are none the less truly beautiful. Their admiration is, or would be if it existed, a truly good thing. Obviously Moore's definition of beauty covers unillustrated abstractions like a mathematical theorem as much as things worked out in sensuous imagery, and it covers anything that is impressive, salient, remarkable, whether in the world of fancy or of fact. It is this curious definition of the beautiful which explains why aesthetic satisfactions occupy such an important place in Moore's account of the 'ideal', of the pure and supreme good. Most of what it is worth while knowing, e.g. the table of Mendeléeff, the theory of general relativity, the life of Ho Chi Minh, etc., is impressive and beautiful in Moore's sense, and Moore is right in holding that the existence, or reality, or truth of what is thus known is only, as it were, a last crowning touch of value added to the other items of value there present. In itself truth is of small importance: it is not facts, but meaningful facts, that are worth knowing. In this judgement Moore concurs with the judgement of those who set and assess examinations at Oxford and Cambridge.

Moore's attempt to sketch a map of the firmament of values is audacious but somewhat eccentric. He opines that

by far the most valuable things which we know or can imagine are certain states of consciousness, which may be roughly described as the pleasures of human intercourse and the enjoyment of beautiful objects. No one probably who has asked himself the question, has ever doubted that personal affection and the appreciation of what is beautiful in Art or Nature, are good in themselves; nor, if we consider strictly what things are worth having *purely for their own sakes*, does it appear probable that anyone will think that anything else has nearly so great a value as the things which are included under these two heads ... what has not been recognized is that it (this) is the ultimate and funda-mental truth of Moral Philosophy. That it is only for the sake of these things that anyone can be justified in performing any public or private duty; that they are the *raison d'être* of virtue; that it is they ... that form the rational ultimate end of human action and the sole criterion of social progress: these appear to be truths that have been generally overlooked (*Principia Ethica*, p. 188)

All Bloomsbury is implicit in these utterances: the pleading is gorgeous, but it fails wholly to persuade. That these are goods for which nothing can be bartered is not in doubt, but they are not the pre-eminent constellations in the value-firmament. It is imposs-ible to exclude from that firmament, or admit merely on quasi-aesthetic grounds, the knowledge, the mind's self-transcending submission to what actually is, to which Plato and Aristotle accorded so high a place: we cannot endorse Moore's supercilious judgement (ibid., p. 199) that 'knowledge, though having little or no value by itself, is an absolutely essential constituent in the highest goods, and contributes immensely to their value'. Nor can we say of the habitual virtue commended by Aristotle 'that to maintain that a virtue which includes no more than this, is good in itself is a gross absurdity. And of this gross absurdity, it may be observed, the Ethics of Aristotle is guilty' (ibid., p. 176).

D

Nor can we agree that the value of certain surpassing cases of courage and compassion is not such as definitely to outweight the evils that call it forth. We cannot say 'There is no reason to think that any actual evil whatsoever would be contained in the Ideal' or that 'we cannot admit the actual validity of any of the arguments commonly used in theodicies' or believe that the supreme good would be attained if we only had to contend in imagination against non-existent evils (ibid., pp. 220–1). Obviously there is something Arcadian, something redolent of the Cambridge backs, in all this, and one can only be struck dumb by the unargued dismissal of so much that other reflective men have thought precious. 'No Cross, no Crown', and 'The unexamined life is not worth living' are valuations as deeply experienced and persuasive as any of those of Moore.

On great evils Moore is more completely persuasive. The first class of these consists in the admiring contemplation of things which are themselves either evil or ugly, and here cruelty and lasciviousness are given as salient instances. We may agree with Moore that cruelty is the most absolute of all evils, and that no theory of valuation can be listened to which subverts or even questions such a judgement, but lasciviousness would require a stronger case to be made against it than that given by Moore who is content to say that 'there are cognitions of organic sensations and perceptions of states of the body, of which the enjoyment is certainly an evil in itself' (ibid., p. 209). The second class of great evils are all cases of the hatred of what is good or beautiful, and that these are great evils, and not in virtue of a tautology, is quite plain. In the third class of great evils Moore puts pain, which rightly occupies a more eminent place among evils than pleasure does among goods. We may, in conclusion, admire Moore for his fine voyage of discovery among the varied territories of value, even if he has failed to explore some thoroughly or has drawn their contours all awry, and even if he has not provided us with anything of a rational method, other than mere intuition, by means of which such exploration can be carried out.

Hastings Rashdall is the second of our chosen British moral philosophers who has developed an axiological view of ethics:

his opinions are set forth in the two impressive volumes of *The Theory of Good and Evil* (1907). Writing at a time when the influence of Bradley hung like a pall over Oxford, neither permitting common-or-garden analysis or genuine Hegelian dialectic, Rashdall was as clear a thinker as the nebulous subject-matter of value would allow him to be, while avoiding the exaggerated atomism of Moore's treatments. Like Moore, Rashdall held that the notion of value or good was the fundamental idea for ethics, and without the trappings of the naturalistic fallacy or the harshly posed distinction between goodness and good things, he refused to identify the good with Pleasure, Virtue, Knowledge, etc., by making it pervade them all alike; there are in fact quite a number of distinct good things which morality must bring together and compare and fit into the ordered pattern of the good life.

The rightness of acts Rashdall explains, like Moore, in terms of productivity of a maximal amount of good, though he avoids the pitfall of saying that this is what 'rightness' means, or of giving any bad reason to show that this is what the content of duty must be. It would, he thinks, be self-evidently immoral to think we can do more than our duty – yet many good men have thought just this – and this must mean that we are always obliged to produce the largest amount of good that it seems possible for us to produce. On the avoidance of evils Rashdall has little or nothing to say, not entering into the question, as Moore does in the case of pain, whether evils may not in some respects behave differently from goods and be governed by distinct principles: the principle tacitly accepted is that evil is simply good in reverse and can in all circumstances be simply cancelled out by countervailing good.

To the whole view that the rightness of acts consists in promoting, or seeking to promote, the greatest possible amount of good open to the agent to produce, Rashdall gives the excellent name of 'ideal utilitarianism', a name much used for a time in describing the thought of Plato and Aristotle. This ideal utilitarianism did not have the unpalatable consequence that right acts and virtuous efforts have a merely instrumental value as producing valuable consequences beyond themselves, as is taught in all forms of hedonistic utilitarianism. A right act or a virtuous effort may contribute its own quota of value to the overall situation, and this may, in many cases, be much more important than the pleasure or just distribution that it effects. It is overall goodness in all its forms, immediate or consequential, which decides rightness or obligatoriness, and there is no reason why an ideal utilitarianism may not sometimes place so high a value on certain actions and efforts as to let them outweigh all consequences that are in any way likely.

As regards our mental access to goodness Rashdall, like Meinong and Moore, makes it a matter of intuitive judgement, and a judgement involving the '*a priori* and purely intellectual idea of value' (*Theory of Good and Evil*, 1 156). But this intuitive judgement is rooted in facts of feeling in a not merely contingent and empirical manner. *At least* it is the case that feelings are the 'subjective index' by means of which we recognise value-properties in things, but it is more than that: 'moral judgements imply facts of feeling as part of their ground' and 'value cannot be recognised as attributable to anything in consciousness which can excite no feeling of pleasure in its possession' (ibid., pp. 153–4). On the other hand, Rashdall also says that value-terms would not mean *nothing* to one incapable of a variety of value-concerned emotions, and that what they meant would still be the 'very essence of the moral judgement' (ibid., p. 170). Rashdall further refuses to believe in *one* specifically moral emotion (ibid., p. 171), and thinks that there are great dangers in believing that there is or must be one. It will lead us to look only to emotionally stirring cases of value and ignore the humdrum commonsensical ones (ibid., p. 173). These statements do not add up to any clear and satisfactory theory of the relations of 'reason and emotion' in the value-judgement, but they at least recognise the unique and peculiar status of a rationality which works through emotions and of an emotionality which has the dispassionate, revelatory quality of an act of reason.

As regards the concrete goods to which Rashdall's *a priori* category of value attaches, they are all held to be actual states of consciousness: 'it is in actual consciousness that value resides and in nothing else' (ibid., p. 65). This account excludes from value anything merely facultative or dispositional, as the virtues, on certain accounts, have been held to be. 'Those who make virtue an end mean by "virtue", virtuous consciousness. . . . And the virtuous consciousness means a consciousness whose volitions and desires are controlled by a rational ideal of life, together with the feelings and emotions inseparably accompanying such volitions and desires' (ibid., p. 65).

The actual states of consciousness to which value attaches are of a wide number of different sorts, or they exhibit a large number of aspects in virtue of which they are more or less valuable. In general, however, they fall into three main groups, of which the highest group consists of a wide number of forms of virtuous consciousness, most of which have been named by tradition, while the lowest group consists of a wide number of forms of pleasurable consciousness, of which pleasure and happiness are the broadly distinguished varieties. But between the virtuous and the pleased forms of consciousness, lie what, for lack of a better word, we may call its cultured states, its states which are part of the 'life of the mind', which revolve about Art, Letters, Learning and the like. The educated Victorian–Edwardian world in which Rashdall moved certainly believed in Morality, Culture and Entertainment as the three distinct forms of what is individually and socially desirable, and they certainly ranked them much as Rashdall does.

Rashdall is, however, very keen that we should not ignore *any* of these main differentiations of value even though there may be some with little capacity to participate in one or other of them. Man is Reason, Feeling and Will and the ideal state for man, and hence also for society, is an ideal state of *all* the three elements in human nature in their ideal relation to one another. Rashdall's utilitarianism is accordingly organic and will not permit simple substitution of one sort of good for another. It is not the human ideal to live only in states of pleasure regardless of their source, nor to eschew all pleasures but those which form part of the highest mental activities: pleasure *qua* pleasure, and the lower as well as the higher pleasure, is indefeasibly part of the human good. In the same way it is not the human ideal to cultivate only the higher forms of virtue and to neglect culture or happiness or both, and Rashdall also makes a point afterwards stressed by Scheler and Hartmann that there can be no virtues of generosity, fairness, courage, etc., unless there are other goods than virtue which these virtues can dispense, distribute, defend, etc. This does not of course mean that the value of these virtues is in any way a function of the more elementary values with which they are concerned. Culture and pleasure without virtue are not, of course, an admissible choice at all, and the sort of value that we call 'aesthetic', while having a peculiar autonomy that Rashdall finds difficult to analyse, can none the less not set itself up against values as a whole – as some aesthetes have tried to make it do – but has a place assigned in that pattern, and one must on each occasion judge how far it can be allowed to go.

But despite his organicism and his doctrine of the non-substitutability of values, Rashdall still professes himself a believer in the 'commensurability' of all values. Though values may to some extent be relative to context, yet in a determinate context it is possible to compare them, and to compare them quantitatively. One valuable goal can in given circumstances be rated as more or less valuable than another, and this sheer quantity of value can in some cases outweigh difference of values which involve 'height'. Thus the integrity of a Chinese mandarin is a higher thing than the freedom from torture and dishonour of a number of European prisoners: none the less it may be right to corrupt the Mandarin to save the Europeans, since there is *more* value thus realised. (It is strange how the forgotten prejudices of the period intrude into an impartial treatise.) Rashdall entirely deprecates the view that there are some values or disvalues so immensely exalted that no amount of a lower value or disvalue can compensate for them. Cardinal Newman tried to defend the Catholic conception of lying as venial, by holding that it would be better for the whole human race to die in agony than for one man to commit a venial act of lying. This judgement, Rashdall mildly asserts, is unacceptable (*Theory of Good and Evil*, ii 43). It may be noted that Rashdall's doctrine of the commensurability of all values does not entail commensurability in terms of a common unit. He thinks, however, that there are cases where it *does* make sense to say that A is n times better than B.

Rashdall mitigates the harshness of the over-rigorous doctrine of the obligatory maximisation of values, and of the denial of works of supererogation, by a doctrine of vocation. It is not everyone's duty to strive for the higher values above the lower on every occasion, since not everyone has a vocation to produce these higher values, or to maintain production of them on all occasions. Those who aspire to heights of culture or of virtue beyond their capacity will bring less value into being than if they had aimed lower: their vocation is in fact to produce and enjoy lower types of value. On this ground and on this alone can we justify the reduction of a man's level of aspiration in the field of duty: it is always one's duty to produce the best of which one is capable in the whole situation of persons and things of which one is a part. This stress on vocation is, of course, very important, but one may doubt whether it deals with the obstinate feeling that one is *not* obliged to maximise value even within the limits of one's vocation, and that the view that one is so ignores the higher kinds of merit.

A remaining point of interest in Rashdall's theory is his excellent treatment of distributive justice in volume I, chapter VIII. Rashdall points out that it is not sufficient that we should maximise good: it is also necessary that we should do so fairly, justly, impartially, without arbitrary inequality. The immense obscurity of the egalitarianism which seems part of the notion of justice is recognised by Rashdall when he says that justice involves no more than 'equality of consideration'. It need not in all circumstances involve equalisation of well-being, nor equalisation of possession of the instruments and opportunities of well-being, nor any sort of straightforward equalisation. Differences of capacity render all this impossible, and so do differences of individual taste and preference, and so too, of course, do abundances and shortages in what is desired. But the sheer vagueness of the general notion of justice does not affect the validity of its inspiration nor

49

the possibility of giving it a concrete meaning in frameworks made definite by nature or by social convention.

Rashdall, however, feels that justice constitutes a grave problem for ideal utilitarianism. For if the maximisation of good is the sole criterion of duty, why should we lay stress on the way good is distributed? Shall we say that the just distribution of good is itself a good of higher order? This view Rashdall rejects, since a higher-order good would be a mere abstraction, and not an actual state of anyone's consciousness. This objection would, however, touch all those higher patterns of good which are spread out over a whole society or even over the consciousness of the same person at different times: a happy life for example, is not concentrated into a single state of consciousness. If there can be genuine welfare of this distributed sort, it is not clear why justly distributed welfare should not be a genuine form of good. Rashdall prefers to balance his books by stressing justice as a *virtue*; an unjust society may realize more good for its members except in respect of the justice of some or all of those members. But Rashdall's doctrine conflicts with his own principle that virtue is always founded on values beyond itself. If there were no such evil as an unjust allocation of good (in a non-willed sense of 'unjust' and 'allocation'), then there could no moral evil in the wills which tolerated such an unjust allocation.

Sir David Ross, the third British moral philosopher we are to study, built his views on the treatments of Moore and Rashdall: he is not, however, a pure axiologist, an ideal utilitarian as they are, but his system none the less includes a considerable infusion of ideal utilitarianism on which we shall mainly lay stress. His two works on ethics, *The Right and the Good* (1930) and *The Foundations of Ethics* (1939) have a certain dull greatness which shines through the crudity of certain of his formulations and the pettifogging character of some of his arguments. The influence of Aristotle and Butler, as well as an unusually wide and deep study of contemporary British, American and continental thought, gives his work a classic quality: he is not afraid to say of certain moral axioms that 'the moral order expressed in these propositions is just as much part of the fundamental nature of the universe (and, we may add, of any possible universe in which there were moral agents at all) as is the spatial or numerical structure expressed in the axioms of geometry or arithmetic. . . . . In both cases we are dealing with propositions that cannot be proved, but that just as certainly need no proof' (*Right and Good*, pp. 29–30).

The doctrine with which the name of Ross is mainly associated is that of *prima facie rightness* or *prima facie duty*. On that view, what we ought to do on a given occasion is always the outcome of a number of distinct 'claims' upon us, each of which would become our full-fledged duty if it were the only claim in the field. Some of these claims are axiological and are rooted in different values and disvalues that we recognise and of which we feel the attraction or repulsion. Among all these we have to seek the ideal utilitarian accommodation recommended by Moore and Rashdall: we must weigh the goods and evils inherent in, or springing from, various possible lines of conduct open to us at the moment, and opt for the line of conduct that will, we consider, contribute the greatest amount of additional good to the universe and the least amount of evil. This ideal utilitarian claim is very important, and is in fact the general background of the life of duty, which develops into our unconditional duty when other special claims are not present.

There are, however, a number of special claims which Ross does not think reducible to any addition of value or reduction of disvalue, but which are felt as right without regard to any amount of good or evil they may contribute to the universe. These claims may be overridden by utilitarian claims of sufficient weight, but there are circumstances in which they will override such utilitarian claims. In *The Right and the Good* Ross lists among such non-utilitarian requirements those (*a*) which demand fidelity to a promise or engagement or tacit understanding arrived at with others; (*b*) those which demand gratitude, and expressions of gratitude, for benefits previously conferred on us by others; (*c*) those which demand the upsetting of a distribution of pleasure or happiness which is not in accord with the merit of those among whom there is such a distribution. Ross also points to such non-utilitarian anomalies as that we are much more stringently bound to avoid injuring others (duty of non-maleficence) than we are bound to promote their positive well-being, and to the curious fact that while we have a duty to improve our own condition as regards virtue and knowledge (duty of self-improvement) we are not obliged to promote our own pleasure. All these special claims relating to whom we have special relations or to special forms of good, are not easily dealt with by the general utilitarian formula of endeavouring to maximise good and minimise evil, but seem to involve an added note of sacredness or stringency: this may be overridden by merely utilitarian claims, which in such a case have a higher, more stringent *prima facie* rightness, but they have in all cases to be considered.

It is not our task here to go into all the arguments for and against the non-axiological claims on which Ross lays such stress. It is arguable that Ross finds it hard to deal with them in an axiological framework because he fails to see that the sort of values with which our more stringent duties are concerned are essentially disvalues rather than positive values, and disvalues of an entirely intrinsic and very grave sort. They are disvalues which as it were question and place in jeopardy the whole fabric of mutual adjustment and accommodation which is the foundation of the moral order, a foundation which all positive values require for their security, and which are not to be put on a level with values and disvalues of the occasion which are as it were, only a loose, changeable superstructure built on the basis in question. Breaches of faith, acts of ingratitude, grossly unequal distributions in a sense rend the whole fabric of our mutual social commitment, defy the moral order and therefore involve an evil much greater than any transitory inconvenience or personal discomfiture. This evil tends to pass unnoticed, since the duties of fidelity, gratitude, veracity, common fairness, etc., which guard against them, do not, if fulfilled, yield goods of any particularly high order. They provide only the foundations, not the pinnacles of the axiological order. Seen in this light, as being concerned with the avoidance of grave underminings and questionings of the whole order of values, the duties in question can be held to have their roots in the grave disvalues which they seek to avoid. They are part of the grave need to minimise evil rather than augment good, which Ross too recognises when he acknowledges the more stringent character of the obligation not to harm over the obligation to benefit or improve. If ideal utilitarianism is allowed to recognise and give full weight to the profound gulf between the good and the bad, and to recognise that the avoidance of evil is in some deep sense more fundamental than the achievement of good, then it will perhaps be possible to bring Ross's duties of special obligation into the fold of an amended ideal utilitarianism.

Ross stresses the non-deducible character of the accommodation of the various duty-claims upon us: we have *prima facie* duties of various sorts, but there is no general principle according to which we can decide which should prevail in a given case. A certain moral perception, to make use of a notion of Aristotle's, alone can cut the Gordian knot. The principle that the more stringent *prima facie* duty should prevail, affords no guidance, and is in fact little more than a tautology, and so is the ideal utilitarian principle that one should always produce the better of two alternative goods. 'When we have to choose between the production of two heterogeneous goods, say knowledge and pleasure, the "ideal utilitarian" theory can only fall back on an opinion, for which no logical basis can be offered, that one of the goods is the greater; and this is no better than a similar opinion that one of two duties is the more urgent' (*The Right and the Good*, p. 23). (One wonders whether there is here even any genuine difference of meaning between the ideal utilitarian and Ross's deontological mode of speaking.) Ross further says that 'the sense of our particular duty in particular circumstances, preceded and informed by the fullest reflection we can bestow on the act in all its bearings, is highly fallible, but it is the only guide we have to our duty' (ibid., p. 42). Where all is so extremely without principle one is inclined to wonder whether Aristotelian talk of 'perception' and the suggestions of a differing amount of value or differing degree of stringency, always present but not always rightly apprehended, are really in place at all. One is inclined to feel sympathy with the modern talk of a *decision* among various general duty- or value-claims. However this all may be, Ross's conception of *prima facie* duty does justice to an all-important fact in the phenomenology of choice: that we are always liable to be faced by a number of distinct calls to realise good or avoid bad, not capable of being reconciled in practice, and not subject to any principle which determines their preferential order. Conflict among such claims and the sheer overriding of one by the other, are part of the structure of value-experience, which is perhaps much what Hartmann meant when he spoke of the 'antinomic' character of the realm of values.

We must turn, however, from Ross's conceptions of 'rightness', to his conceptions of value or goodness which are more central for our purpose. *Part*, at least, of our moral life consists in deciding which is the more valuable or less disvaluable of a number of realisable or avoidable states of things, which may all be our 'objectives' of pursuit or avoidance. Ross believes that *both* rightness and goodness are unanalysable properties, the former pertaining specifically to acts, the latter to states of affairs generally. We can specify the various possible *grounds* of rightness and goodness, but this is not to say what these properties themselves are. We need not repeat our criticisms of Moore's doctrine of the naturalistic fallacy: obviously they apply here. Ross holds that our judgement as to the goodness or relative goodness of various sorts of things always *expresses* our personal attitudes to the things concerned but that it never *means or refers to* those attitudes: what it means or refers to is a property that has nothing to do with anyone's attitude to anything, and which belongs purely to the state of affairs under consideration. 'What we *express* when we call an object good is our attitude towards it, but what we *mean* is something about the object itself and not about our attitude towards it. When we call an object good we are commending it, but to commend is not to say that we are commending it, but to say that it has a certain character, which we think it would have whether we were commending it or not' (*Foundations of Ethics*, p. 255). The peculiar use of 'expression' and 'meaning' which here occurs is borrowed from Meinong, but Ross does not develop anything like Meinong's full doctrine of emotional presentation.

He only says that an emotional attitude is *in some manner* essential to a judgement of value, but that such a judgement is none the less purely intellectual, fact-stating, truth-directed. Ross, like Moore, thinks that so much is required to make value-dispute and argument possible.

If we now turn to Ross's views as to the main sorts of things that are good, we find him more or less following Rashdall in first accepting *three* main divisions of goodness: the goodness of virtuous disposition, the goodness of knowledge and opinion, and the goodness of being pleased or happy. But fourthly and more hesitantly Ross accepts, as Rashdall was not willing to accept, as an independent, higher-order good, 'the apportionment of pleasure and pain to the virtuous and the vicious respectively', a non-moral good upon whose recognition and pursuit the moral good of justice depends (*The Right and the Good*, p. 138). Ross's view of the relations of these various sorts of good is more abstractly moralistic than Rashdall's: he conceives that, while there can be graded comparisons of value *in* each of the three main departments of value, there is only a total difference of grade among the three departments themselves. This means that all cases of virtue are more valuable than all cases of knowledge and pleasure, and that all cases of knowledge are more valuable than all cases of pleasure. The weakest virtuous stirring is necessarily worth more than the most powerful act of intellectual penetration and the greatest of pleasures. One is reminded of Cardinal Newman's preference of universal but innocent agony to a single venial sin, and of Rashdall's rejection of it. It is, however, the logic of the doctrine which on reflection, disquiets Ross: he does not see how one scale of magnitude can begin totally above the infinite levels possible on another, a problem which a mathematician would not find serious. He therefore takes the view that the impossibility of grading items belonging to different scales lies in the fact that they embody different *senses* of goodness or value. The goodness of virtue and knowledge consists in (or is at least bound up with) the fact that they are fit objects of *admiration*, whereas the goodness of certain pleasures, which Ross restricts to the pleasures of *others*, is that they are fit objects of satisfaction. These doctrines are far from clear. That the goodness of virtue and knowledge is indefinable and yet is capable of being 'paraphrased' as being a fit object of admiration (*Foundations of Ethics*, p. 253) is not wholly easy to comprehend, nor yet why pleasure, which is a fit object of satisfaction, should be without such an indefinable property. But by these doctrines Ross maintains his moralism, even if he is forced to put intellectual values into the same class as moral values, and is also able to draw a very moralistic distinction between one's own pleasures and those of others, the former not being good in any ethically significant sense, and so something that we are not obliged to produce at all.

Ross then goes on to many interesting analyses of moral value, grading virtue according to the *motives* which inspire conduct. The highest of such motives is the desire to do one's duty, the next highest the desire to achieve something good, in so far as it is good, beneath which lie many motives directed to valuable ends but without any conscious direction to their value. Ross does not think that mixed motivation necessarily detracts from moral excellence provided the highest motives could do the trick alone: if this is the case, the addition of other good motives augments the virtue. And Ross does not think that moral value diminishes if a choice comes wholly easy, provided that the same choice would have been made had circumstances *not* made it easy.

Our criticism of many details of Ross's teaching must not be allowed to obscure the impressive coherence of the whole, and its faithfulness to many of the finer shades of valuation. Ross is at all times alive to the most minute nuances of the moral judgement, and to complex distinctions which it is only too easy to ignore or minimise. His treatment, like that of Moore and Rashdall, certainly shows that, despite endless points of controversy, there is an ordered system of values and disvalues which comes to light in moral reflection and discourse, and that there is a worthwhile philosophical enterprise which investigates this ordered system.

IV. SCHELER AND HARTMANN

In the present chapter we shall sketch the contents of two major German contributions to value-theory, works which not only study the general logic of value-discourse, but which also draw up a comprehensive map of the value-firmament, an ordered setting forth of the different sorts of things that can be held to be good or bad in some cogently valid fashion, and which can arguably be placed in cogently valid relations to one another. These works are Max Scheler's *Formalism in Ethics and the Material Value-Ethic*, first published in Husserl's *Jahrbuch für Philosophie und phänomenologische Forschung* (*Journal for Philosophy and Phenomeno-logical Research*) in 1913 and 1914, but not as yet translated into English, and Nicolai Hartmann's *Ethics*, published in German in 1926, and in an English translation by Stanton Coit in 1932. Both works have a certain sweeping splendour: they consider many questions that Anglo-Saxon moral philosophers never raise (though ordinary Anglo-Saxons often consider them) and they see all these questions in a systematic interrelatedness which is also largely foreign to Anglo-Saxon thought. On the whole they leave one with the impression that, however difficult it may be to lay bare the rationale of value-research, it is none the less something that *can* be undertaken, and that can be made to yield results neither emptily analytic nor arbitrarily personal. Both abound in loosely stated and poorly substantiated insights, which do not always form a coherent pattern. Their analyses do not, however, remain obstinately on the fringe of what is worth considering, attached to the false dogma that the most obvious truisms are also those that will yield the richest harvest of truth and light, and their easy inconsistency means that they do not remain obdurately wedded to wrong methods and basic misconceptions, which lead repeatedly to the same *impasse*. Socrates and Moore were both philosophers of the most august greatness, but we may be glad that not all philosophers chopped logic as finely and as vainly as they did. Scheler and Hartmann both think darkly and nebulously, but since the realm of values is itself darkly nebulous rather than classically clear, and resembles a Teutonic Valhalla more than a Greek Olympus, we have perhaps more to learn from them than from moral philosophers all too obstinately clear-cut and consistent.

Max Scheler's work on ethics is only one of his immensely original, penetrating studies of the human person in relation to the world, to other human persons, and to a supercosmic, eternal something, which, whether real or unreal, transcends the cosmos and the conscious beings in it. The foundations of his thought lie in Husserl, and he is everywhere concerned to describe matters as they appear or are given to consciousness, and not to allow scientific of metaphysical theories to undermine or overturn the conscious appearances. Thus whatever the obscure processes, physical, physiological and psychological, that may have led to our complex vision of the world as it stands arrayed around us, the fact is that it is a world that includes things as well as sensations, situations as well as things, other conscious beings as well as ourselves, inner states as well as outer acts, values as well as valueless facts, and a numinous culmination which gathers together and unifies all phenomena, whether or not we treat it as an illusion. Towards such appearances we must be loyal, however much theorists may assure us that 'all they really are' is movements of atoms, excitations of neurons, patterns of behaviour, linguistic constructions, etc: the content of such theories is less solid than the appearances they set out to explain. Scheler was, however, an early pupil of Husserl's, much more influenced by the *Logische Untersuchungen* (*Logical Investigations*, trans. J. N. Findlay (Routledge, 1970)) of 1899–1901 than by the phenomenological writings that began to pour forth in 1913. His point of view is accordingly realistic rather than idealistic, and while the phenomena which make up the experienced world are necessarily set up for the subject in certain characteristic psychic acts, there is no suggestion that what is thus set up may not also, in limiting cases, coincide, and be known to coincide, with things as they in themselves authentically are. Scheler's whole book is in fact part of an attempt of German thought to free itself from the influence of Kant, from Kantian 'constructivism' in epistemology and from Kantain rigorism and imperativism in ethics. The attempt may be adjudged vain, since these sides of Kant still dominate German thought.

Scheler, like Hartmann, is concerned to put emotion, rather than cold intellectual grasp, at the centre of value-experience: it is in and through our feelings that objects and states come before us as endowed with worthwhileness and counterworthwhileness, and without feelings this essential side of things could not get through to us at all. It is all-important, however, that we should have a correct theory of the sort of feelings that are concerned in value-experience, and that we should not assimilate them to the states, conditions, *Zustände*, sensational modifications that we merely live through, without intrinsically directing ourselves to objects in and through them, or which, if they are afterwards connected with objects, are so connected in a merely extrinsic, causal manner. The feelings that are important for value-experience are essentially 'intentional', directed feelings: they discharge themselves upon objects rather than are merely produced by them. And this intentional directedness is never casual nor at random, but is always the appropriate *answer* to what the object is given to us as being, so that the same situation in which we direct feelings towards an object is also one in which the object reveals itself as being in some way suited to the feelings we direct towards it, or in other words as having a value. The connections between intrinsically directed feelings and objects having something that suits them have, further, the universal cogency which stamps them as *a priori*: they are not grounded inductively on what we uniformly find to be the case in beings like ourselves, but are lived through as ineluctable, as appropriate, as having the same sort of force as pure logic. To quote Scheler:

It is our *whole* spiritual life – not merely our objective cognition and thought in the sense of a knowledge of being – that involves *pure* acts and pure act-principles, i.e. acts and principles independent of the facts of our human organization, in essence and content. The emotional side of our spirit, our feeling, preference, love, hate, willing, also has its own *a priori* content, which it does not borrow from thinking, and which ethics must set forth in entire independence from logic. There is an *a priori ordre du cœur* or *logique du cœur* as Blaise Pascal tellingly puts it. (*Formalism*, p. 59)

Or again:

A feeling of anger arises in me and runs its course, a feeling which certainly has no intentional, original bond with the thing *about* which I am angry. The idea, the thought, or rather the objects given in them, that I at first perceived, conceived or thought, arouse my anger, and only afterwards – very quickly in normal cases – do I relate my feelings to these objects, always through my idea of them. I certainly 'apprehend' nothing in such anger . . . The situation is quite different when I rejoice or grieve over or about something . . . The words 'over' and 'about' reveal in speech that in such rejoicing or grieving objects are not first apprehended, *over* which I rejoice, etc., but that they rather have stood before me already, not merely as things perceived, but as things coloured by certain value-predicates given in feeling. The value-qualities given in the valuation in question intrinsically *demand* certain qualities in such 'response-reactions', just as these last in their turn achieve their target in them. (Ibid., p. 268)

The passages quoted reveal all the penetration and confusion of Scheler's treatment. There is no developed theory, as in Meinong, as to how an emotional reaction, merely because it is directed or appropriate, can mediate an apprehension of value in that to which it is directed. Nor is it clear that anger is not often as intrinsically directed and appropriate as rejoicing and grieving. Moreover the whole analysis proves too much. Intentionality is not necessarily the same as justifiability: to be specifically directed to some object, is not to be nor to seem justifiably so directed. One good reason for believing in objective value-predicates is that we do not *always* feel that our emotional intentionality has anything justified about it: sometimes it appears merely 'personal'. The fact that we *sometimes* feel a peculiar correctness and appropriateness in our directed emotions at least provides an argument (if not a truly clinching one) for holding there to be some objective peculiarity in what we feel about in such cases.

It is interesting, in view of Scheler's emotional theory of valuation, to note his reaction to the emotive theory of value-discourse which, though only launched in Anglo-Saxon countries in the thirties, is clearly set forth and pondered by Scheler in the second decade of the century, and given the name of 'ethical nominalism'. Scheler writes: 'If after experiencing a pain I cry "Ow", this "Ow", is not directed to the experienced pain as when I say "I am feeling pain": it simply expresses such pain. . . . Just so the sentences "This is good (bad)" do not report the content of an inner experience as taking place or as having taken place nor communicate it to others: they only *express* certain acts of emotion and desire' (ibid., p. 169). And again: 'In place of the involuntary expressions of desire and feeling, which make up the most primitive sense of the so-called value-judgement, we later encounter the *voluntary intimation* of such acts with the intention to arouse a similar desire and feeling in others' (ibid., p. 170). Scheler refutes such emotivism by holding that there is a 'distinction of essence' between merely responding emotionally to something or desiring others to do so (on the one hand), and really judging something to be good, beautiful, etc. (on the other). This distinction points to a value-predicate in the objects which, though essentially evocative of feeling, is not the same as any feeling it evokes, or any power to evoke such feeling (ibid., pp. 173–4).

We must, however, turn from Scheler's general doctrine of *a priori* emotionality, to the detailed content that he connects with it. He first states such simple-minded axioms as that the existence of a value is itself a value, the non-existence of such a value being (presumably) an equal negative value, whereas the existence of a negative value is itself a negative value, its non-existence being (presumably) an equal value. The writing-off of negative values (disvalues) as the mere absence of values, enables Scheler to work out his whole map of values in terms of positive values. Clearly Scheler has not realised the positive nature of badness, and its non-equivalence to the mere absence of good. Some inkling of this truth, however, filters through in the doctrine that an 'ought', an obligation, while it always derives from a value, is none the less *primarily* concerned with the non-existence of the *disvalue* whose absence is tantamount to the value in question. 'It is therefore the case that a positive value underlies every ought-proposition, a value that it itself never can embrace. For what ought in general to be is never primarily the being of what is good, but only the non-being of what is evil' (*Formalism*, p. 213). This proposition would only make full sense if the non-being of an evil were something different from the being of a good, as it in fact plainly is.

From this doctrine Scheler goes on to make many points in opposition to Kant. An ethics, he holds, that makes 'ought' or duty central, must always of necessity have a merely negative, critical character. 'We see from this', he says, 'that every imperativistic ethic, i.e. every ethic that starts out from the thought of duty as the *most original* ethical phenomenon, and endeavours to reach the ideas of good and bad, virtue and sin, from this starting-point, must throughout be of a merely negative, critical and repressive character' (ibid., p. 215). There are natures that like to approach the sphere of value from this indirect, negative, dutiful angle, but Scheler considers it a defect that they have to do so. (As does Kant also, we may remark, in his doctrine of a holy will.) All this being assumed, it is only to be expected that Scheler will be unfavourable to a need- or desire-analysis of value or valuation. 'It is not the case', he writes,

as the need-theory of value and valuation supposes . . . that anything, an *X*, only has value in so far as it satisfies a need. The valuableness of anything does not mean that a mere lack, the objective-correlate of the need-experience, is removed, that a value-vacuum is as it were filled, a hole stopped up. Rather does the feeling of lack presuppose that the *positive* value of the missing good is first given in feeling, in so far, that is, as we do not have a merely *undirected* pressure that does not at all qualify to be called a need. (Ibid., p. 364)

Scheler has of course not proved his point. Plainly there are cases where something is primarily missed rather than positively cherished, and cases where something is primarily cherished and only secondarily missed, if indeed it is missed at all. The most positively precious things are all arguably dispensable. In the absence of any previous, thoroughgoing discussion of these matters, other than that of Meinong, whom Scheler did not read carefully, we may pardon Scheler for his rather poor axiomatisation.

At a stage more concrete, Scheler holds that values form a one-dimensional continuum unambiguously ordered as higher and lower: like Brentano he believes in an irreducible act of *preference* (*Vorziehen*) which is the appropriate medium through which this difference impresses itself on us. He then gives a series of criteria, of somewhat doubtful acceptability, of the higher or lower standing of certain values. Higher values are more enduring than lower ones – a counter-argument for the fleeting, dependent character of higher values might very well have been offered – they are less plainly anyone's special property and so are less diminished when shared, they are more fundamental – again an argument in the opposite direction would have been possible – they yield a *deeper* sort of satisfaction without which lower satisfactions do not really satisfy, and they are less relative to person and situation, more truly absolute, than lower values (ibid., pp. 88–98). The bearers of value are divided into a large number of classes: there are values attaching to persons and values attaching to things, values for self and values for another, values of acts, functions and reactions, of dispositions, deeds and consequences, of intentional and non-intentional experiences, of fundaments, forms and relations, of things for their own sake and of things for something else's sake, etc. As Aristotle would say, all these are good in differing but related senses. Scheler further elaborates an ascending scale of 'value-modalities' which is not unlike the scales of Ross. At the bottom of the scale are the values of the agreeable, ranging from those of mere coenaesthetic bodily agreeableness, through those of unlocalised 'mind-joys' and 'mind-sorrows', up to very lofty forms of spiritual blessedness or despair. Above these hedonic values lie the very Germanic values of *vitality*, values of activity and repose, of energy and exhaustion, of health and disease, as also of the noble and the ignoble: the distinction between nobler and baser forms of existence runs through the whole biological order. Above the vital values lie spiritual (*geistige*) values, which divide familiarly into values of aesthetic enjoyment, of moral participation and of intellectual penetration, and above these again lie the values which express different forms of personal *sanctity*. It is worth while pointing out, as Scheler does, that holiness is an ineliminable upper limit to the value-continuum: it helps to inspire and justify dogmatic religion, rather than being a mere offshoot of the latter. We look in the direction of the holy before some object, often quite inadequate, seems to exemplify it.

In his practical use of this ascending scale of values, Scheler stresses an important principle afterwards taken over by Hartmann: that the higher values cannot be independently pursued, but that they arise 'on the back' of a pursuit of lower values. It is not by seeking to be virtuous or cultivated or scientific, least of all by seeking to be holy, that we become these excellent things: we become them by pursuing and diffusing the lower goods in which it is proper to 'lose ourselves'. Not to achieve such a loss of self, is to corrupt, not to realise, the higher values: in the moral sphere, it is to achieve *Pharisaism* rather than true moral goodness. To Scheler the whole Kantian cult of pure duty is definitely Pharisaic: if one cannot be zealous about other lesser things than duty and purity of will, e.g. the happiness and equal opportunity of others, one cannot be zealous about these latter things at all. Scheler's doctrine is, of course, as exaggeratedly puritanical as the Kantian doctrine: if Kant pushes us towards common kindness while directing us to keep our will fixed on higher moral abstractions, Scheler pushes us towards higher moral abstractions while directing us to keep our will firmly fixed on soup-kitchens or ventures in adult education. Plainly it is possible to aspire to personal culture, virtue and sanctity without rending them from their necessary soil in the pursuit of lower, more foundational goods. But that all such higher goods presuppose lower, foundational goods is an important moral theorem which has been only too often ignored in the long past history of emptily formal treatments of duty or virtue, and of crudely material hedonistic systems.

In the concluding Sixth Section of his work on Ethics Scheler writes abundantly regarding the nature of a person, and of the relation of value to personality. A person is much more than an epistemological subject, and is not merely an abstract point from which mental acts radiate. It is a kind of unity which is *itself* differentiated and totally present in all the acts that we attribute to it, and outside of which they would not be conceivable: it is also a kind of unity which diffuses itself through bodily as well as mental acts, and thereby acquires a seeming diremption into parts external to parts. The essential *Ineinander* or mutual interpenetration of the acts of the person, means, further, that the person is not only *not* intrinsically diffused in space, but also *not* intrinsically successive in time. Its relations to temporality, like those it has to spatiality, are due to its immersion in body. The person is, further, never present to itself in the sense of being an object to its own acts: it *experiences* its unity and pervasive identity rather than envisages these in objectified fashion. These positions are by no means new, and, even if they are in some sense unquestionably true, Scheler has certainly not given them an acceptably lucid sense nor freed them from absurd exaggerations.

It is in the ethical sphere, however, that the person, as opposed to the subject plays its full part, and all values are values for, or of the person. Scheler puts the responsible, adult, sane, normal person in the centre of the axiological picture, and is even prepared to talk as if, in certain phases of value-development, women and slaves, not to mention children and animals, are rightly regarded as sub-persons. There are, of course, certain values which are universal in the sense of not being geared to the distinguishing peculiarities of this or that person or sort of person, but Scheler, like Rashdall, holds to the doctrine of an essentially vocational aspect of truly concrete values, a being tailored to the needs and capacities of the individual person. In this doctrine Scheler is of course setting himself up against the formal universalism of Kant. Scheler writes:

If every 'ought' can only be a genuine moral 'ought' in so far as it rests on insight into objective values, there is also the possibility of evident insight into a good which has reference to an individual person written into its objective essence and value-content, and whose accompanying 'ought' therefore *calls upon* this person and this person alone, regardless as to whether the same call is heard by others or not. ... What is intrinsically good is good 'for me' in the sense that, in the specific material content of this intrinsic good (descriptively put), there is an experienced reference to me, an experienced index that proceeds from this content and points to 'me', that as it were says 'For you'. (*Formalism*, p. 510)

What holds for the individual, holds also for a given moment in the individual's life, or for the particular society to which the individual belongs: all have individual vocations, which are not subsumable under any general principle.

Scheler devotes a great deal of space to the values which are the vocation of *social* as opposed to individual persons: though they realise themselves in and through individual persons, he thinks it right to grant them their own personality. This is even true of the atomistic type of society in which every individual mistrusts and uses every other, though here there is an element of fiction in the 'personality' in question. This is not, however, the case in regard to the highest society, the universal communion of sanctified persons, which remains a necessary idea, whether or not it is satisfactorily embodied in this or that actual church. 'The unity of the church, despite the possible contemporary plurality of social culture-persons. . . . is likewise an *a priori* proposition. The inclusive solidarity *of all possible* finite persons in my salvation, and of my salvation in the salvation of all finite persons, lies in the essence of a total intention directed to the value of all things in the absolute sphere of being and value' (ibid., p. 571).

Such extended construction in spheres deemed mystical and reactionary will not be pleasing to the liberal Anglo-Saxon mind: it is, however, questionable whether this mind, with its hundred clear-cut, dogmatic diremptions, could ever achieve a comprehensive understanding of the firmament of values, or of any inclusive or ultimate matter. More serious questions arise in regard to Scheler's method of investigation. How can we justify the innumerable intuitively based utterances which make up his book, utterances for which so little supporting argument is offered? And how can Scheler explain the existence of maps of value widely differing from his own? Scheler's intuitive method admits the existence of value-delusions and errors, but there is no systematic treatment of their types and sources. At one point only does he indicate a principal source of value-error: the *resentment* which leads one to overvalue one's own achievements and enjoyments, and to undervalue achievements and enjoyments which lie beyond one's range. It is this resentment which makes those

who do the right thing with difficulty and sacrifice, undervalue
the achievements of those who do it with ease, which makes men
see merit in difficulty, sacrifice and even weakness. It is this
resentment which prefers acts done painfully out of duty to acts
done freely out of love, again a point scored against Kant. It is
this resentment which exalts struggle, and connects civilization
with the facing of challenges. Scheler, like Nietzsche, from whom
the notion of resentment is borrowed, will have none of all this.
The luminous values of his empyrean require no dark shadows to
set them off. But it is by no means clear that the need for challenge
and contrast in the value-world can be wholly set down to the
malign workings of resentment: without them, it may be argued,
there could not be values at all.

Hartmann's work on *Ethics*, to which we now turn, is divided
into three main parts, the first concerned with valuation and
value in general, the second with the detailed pattern of the value-
firmament, and the last, riddled with inconsistencies, with the
problem of Free Will. We shall confine ourselves to the first two
parts of the work, which alone concern axiological ethics.

Hartmann takes over, without much added analysis or criticism,
Scheler's doctrine of a logic of the heart. The organ through
which the rich distinctions and structure of the world of value
come home to us is Feeling, and there is an emotional *a priori*,
parallel but not reducible to the *a priori* governing theoretical
fields. Hartmann tellingly points out, much as Hutcheson had done
in the eighteenth century, how widely ranging is the scope of our
feelings, and how vastly wider than the scope of our action or
practical decision. We react approvingly or disapprovingly to acts,
characters and states of affairs remote in space and time which it
is quite beyond our practical power to affect, we react similarly
to things imaginary or even impossible, and we are always
emotionally sensitive to strains of good or bad, better or worse, in
the things around us, even though what we feel about has nothing
to do with us, and does not fall within the range of our practical
business. Nor is it by constituting ourselves imaginary heroes or
policemen or busybodies or creators that we thus respond to the
light and shade in the world: we may remain inert, but we

continue to feel, and sometimes feel seriously about things, as seriously as when practical issues are at stake. Hartmann is far from approving the Anglo-Saxon opinion, plainly having its roots in a particular temperament, that it is only committed *action* that shows what we *sincerely* value or care for. Hartmann then glides, with little more difficulty than Scheler, to the view that the emotional impressions which objects make upon us are also in some way revelations of their intrinsic nature, and that the peculiar stirrings we discharge upon objects also set before us, sometimes in illusory fashion, values and disvalues and 'oughts' which are in no sense matters of feeling, but which inhere in the cosmos or in the possibility of a cosmos. The fact that we only *sometimes* feel that our emotional responses have this objective warrant, that there are purely-personal-seeming as well as objective-seeming values – the preciousness of some keepsake as opposed to the preciousness of truth – and that objects are frequently shifted from one of these cadres to the other, is a point on which Hartmann lays no stress, all-important as it is for the whole of value-analysis.

Hartmann is as entrenchedly opposed to Kant as is Scheler, and, while believing profoundly in an emotional *a priori*, he is concerned to strip this notion of any subjective associations. The axiological *a priori* is all 'out there', an ideal framework of self-existent generalities which we discover and do not make, and which imposes itself on our feeling as the particularities of nature do on our senses or as the generalities of mathematics do on our understanding. Hartmann borrows from Husserl the Platonising belief that there is a direct experience or vision of species, of eidetic universals, as much as of concrete particulars, and that, while our insight into such species and their relations rests in the first instance on experience of particulars and their various 'sides' or aspects, it in no sense reduces to the latter. To understand what it is to be angry or good is an act of pure *ideation* which is quite independent of our ability to illustrate or even recognise anger or goodness in particular cases, a view which has the unmistakable warrant of introspection. It is through our emotional responses that we can become aware, in the first instance, of values in things, and, at a higher remove, of values as such. This doctrine needs to be supplemented by the view that it is through a peculiar psychological tension or pressure that we become aware of the 'ought-to-beness' which derives from and attends upon values, a tension or pressure which is not to be confused with the ought-to-beness which it makes evident to the mind.

Hartmann has a variety of deeply interesting, if not always wholly convincing, views regarding the realm of values which we must now set forth very briefly. He does not, in the first place, believe in a single, uniform essence of value or goodness which acquires specificity only through association with specific 'materials' or descriptive contents, the typical view of Anglo-Saxon analysis. He believes in an infinite variety of *species* of goodness or value (and of course of disvalue) which go with certain variations in material or descriptive content. In this opinion he accords with certain Anglo-Saxon intuitionists, e.g. Ross, who thinks that pleasure and virtue are good in different senses. But for Hartmann there are not merely these broad differences of sense in our value-references, and differently virtuous men will, e.g. the Hellenic and the Christian, be virtuous or good in radically different manners, these differences in virtue being differences in what we may call their axiological aura and not merely in what they do or tend to do. Hartmann further adheres to the somewhat exaggerated view, also defended in Plato's *Lysis*, that what one is really feeling about in a given case shows itself, on reflection, to be always a value *in specie* and never any instance or 'bearer' of such a value. This would entail that it is only *for the sake of* her generic or specific wifely virtues that one can value one's wife, and not as being the individual *bearer* of such excellences. The term 'bearer' is characteristically chosen: the individual becomes a mere peg, as it were, upon which valuable characters hang, a position remote from the extreme 'personalism' of Scheler.

Hartmann believes, like Scheler, that some values are 'given to axiological feeling' as unquestionably 'higher' than others. Thus moral values, the values of voluntary acts and dispositions, are unquestionably higher than 'goods-values' or values of welfare, and some moral values, e.g. those of friendship or loyalty, are unquestionably higher than others, e.g. those of mere veracity. Hartmann stresses the fact that this dimension of 'height' is correlated with peculiar emotional differences: higher values exact a different *Wertantwort* or value-response than do lower ones. There is plainly a deep deference, a Kantian *Achtung*, in our attitude to the higher values which is absent from our attitude towards lower ones. Hartmann leaves it an open question whether there are any general criteria of this valuational 'height', but he rejects as too simple the criteria enumerated by Scheler. It is further clear to Hartmann that 'height' does not represent the *only* dimension in which values order themselves. Many values fall into entirely different orders, and regarding these it is not possible to say that one is higher or lower than the other. There is no clear sense, for example, in saying that aesthetic values are higher or lower than moral values. Hartmann further points out that the realm of value is dominated by a dimension which is to some extent the inverse of the dimension of height, and to which he gives the name of the 'strength' of value. Strong values are those whose *non*-realisation represents a graver disvalue than that of weaker values, and whose ignoring or violation by a voluntary agent represents a graver offence than is the case with weaker values. But such strong values are also in general *lower* values, whereas weaker values tend to be higher. As Hartmann sensibly says: 'A loss of material good is in general a more serious matter than a loss of spiritual goods. A threat to life and limb is the gravest threat, but mere life is not on that account the highest good. . . . Aesthetic is far higher than material pleasure . . . and yet a man strives much more for the latter as long as he does not have it.' Turning to moral value he writes 'that murder, theft and all real crimes are felt to be the most grievous moral transgressions is due to this, that the justice they violate is based on the most elementary of goods-values . . . Hence the unique moral importance of justice. The importance does not attach to its height but its strength.' And again: 'If we compare the highest moral values, for instance radiant virtue or personal love with justice, the twofold relation becomes immediately evident. A neglect of radiant virtue and love exposes no one to radical dangers, a person who is incapable of them is not on that account a bad man.' Hartmann holds therefore that there is a dimension of strength of value concerned not so much with 'the actualization of positive values as with the avoidance of disvalues', and that this dimension is to a large extent independent of the dimension of height, though in general it operates inversely. 'It is this dimension of strength of value which is mainly considered in the severe prohibitions of certain moral codes, and which many philosophers seek to extend to all morality. But morality,' says Hartmann, 'shows a double face – its symbol is the head of Janus. It sets up a backward looking claim to the more elementary values, and a forward looking claim to the higher values.' Perversion results if *either* of these dimensions is exclusively regarded. It is as wrong to think only in terms of crying positive evils and their obligatory avoidance, as to think only in terms of 'higher things' and to ignore such crying positive evils. Would that this Janus-wisdom had filtered down to the conventional puritans of our ethical tradition. (See *Ethics*, vol. II, English translation, pp. 449–59.)

The many-dimensional realm of values has, however, a necessary relation to realisation which Hartmann expresses in terms of the notion of 'ought' (*Sollen*). Whether or not values are instantiated, it is part of the being of all values in some sense to demand instantiation, and this part of their being Hartmann calls their ideal ought-to-beness. Values, *qua* values, have an interior content distinct from such ideal ought-to-beness – being valuable is, in other words, not simply being what ought to be – but the two notions entail one another. Such ideal ought-to-beness is not always a case of ought-to-be-doneness, since many values are not realisable by action, and some even transcend the possible, and are in principle unrealisable whether by action or in any other manner. This ideal ought-to-beness, however, gives rise to what Hartmann calls a positive ought-to-beness whenever the real sphere is out of step with the ideal sphere of values, and this positive ought-to-beness is experienced as a *tension* by conscious practical beings, a tension which may take the form of a more or less ardent wish or, in some cases, of a practical resolution or an actual performance. This tension, which in certain cases amounts to the voice of duty, is the medium, but only the medium, through which positive ought-to-beness is apprehended: those who experience the tension also know the nature of the ought-to-beness which is what is given in and through the tension, and it does not make sense to ask what in itself such an ought-to-beness is or means.

Hartmann believes, further, that though the ought-to-beness of values is in no sense subjective, it is only through subjects, and in fact only through the special subjects called 'persons', that it gains any purchase on the world. Conscious practical subjects become aware of values through feeling, they experience their ought-to-beness in the tension of necessary desire, they may then be moved to think out plans for realising such values in actual situations, and such plans may then be put into action so that what ought to be comes to coincide with what actually is. Outside of conscious practical persons the realm of values is, however, held to be without influence on the actual world. Hartmann does not believe in a Platonic influence of the Good on the arrangement of things in nature, nor in any form of unconscious Aristotelian teleology. He puts before us the very Germanic picture of Man as having a unique 'demiurgic' vocation, as being *the one channel* through which what is good can become part and parcel of what actually exists. And not only is this the one channel for such influence, it is also a channel that may or may not be used, according as a man freely decides to realise or not to realise such values as he feels. (Hartmann's views on freedom are, however, a sad nest of obscure contradictions.)

Values, moreover, according to Hartmann, are radically different from categories, since it is never the case that they *must* be embodied in the world, only that they make a claim, inspire an effort, suggest a line leading to such embodiment. If nature worked unconsciously toward what is good, or if man necessarily realised the highest when he saw it, and was able to realise it, then values would be categories, part and parcel of the structure of the universe. The non-categorial nature of values is, further, shown by *their intrinsically antinomic character*. What is good, Hartmann tells us, necessarily lies in a large number of incompatible directions, and it is intrinsically impossible that *all* of these should be followed out into realisation. One cannot, for example, achieve pure simplicity and variegated richness in the same thing or occasion, and yet *both* incontestably make claims upon us, and ought *both* to be realised. The realm of values, in fact, always imposes a logically impossible task upon us: we are to achieve each and all of a large number of things which yet *cannot* all be achieved together. In practice, of course, we sacrifice one good to another, or we make compromises and accommodations among goods, or we realise one here and another there, and so on. This does not affect the fact that all such practical accommodations necessarily override the claims of certain values, and everywhere consummate something that in some respects ought not to be. And Hartmann even thinks that there is a sense in which we are always 'guilty' in such antinomic situations, guilty for not having realised *all* the good things which are yet such that they *cannot* all be realised. What Hartmann here teaches would to many seem absurd, and certainly he uses the term 'guilt' in a curious, unacceptable, Germanic manner. It remains arguable that the doctrine of the antinomic character of all values is profoundly true to our value-experience. What is self-contradictory certainly makes no sense in theory: there are no states of affairs that can ever make it true. But, contrary to what is generally thought, what is self-contradictory makes sense in practice: we are in fact obliged to strive towards value-accommodations to which full reality can never be given. Even Kant saw this when he held that only in eternity could we conform to the demands of the categorical imperative. The whole of our moral life is riddled with situations where we have to behave as if something were the case which probably is not and cannot be so, and only a very shallow morality results from full adaptation to what is actual or possible. (Not that this last is not also a necessary part or 'side' of morality, not fully reconcilable with the other part.) To be a 'knight of the ideal' may not accord with contemporary Marxist and similar fashions, but it may be argued that one will not achieve any morality at all if one aspires to less.

Hartmann, further, attempts a curious analysis of 'oughtness' in its relation to actuality and necessity, thereby making an eccentric but illuminating contribution to modal logic. An 'ought' is a necessity that has, by some strange mischance, been loosed from that close connection with actuality and possibility that other necessities entail. Two plus two *must* amount to four, and it is also a fact and a possibility that they should in all cases do so. A man must (in the sense of 'should') be wise as a serpent and gentle as a dove, but this does not mean that he will in fact be both of these things, or even that it is *possible* for him to be both of them. 'Ought' in fact goes with 'cannot' as often as 'can', and the ultimate 'oughts' are cases of 'cannot' rather than 'can'. Modal logicians are unlikely to incorporate Hartmann's suggestions into their treatments of deontic logic: the fact remains that he has pointed to a profound analogy between two senses of 'must' which also goes paired with an equally profound difference.

Hartmann couples his view of the strange, complex topography of value with a special view as to why we map it so inadequately. We do so because our feeling for value has a narrowness, an *Enge*, like the narrowness of conscious attention. To be deeply cognisant of the worthwhileness of certain things is necessarily to let the worthwhileness of other things become lost in the margin, and this is particularly so when the things in question are widely disparate or perhaps practically incompatible. If our whole life is built around certain values, it is unlikely that we shall be highly sensitive to values remote from these or even tending in a contrary direction. But the focus of valuation, like the focus of conscious attention, compensates for its narrowness by its tendency to shift, and it is by such a 'wandering' of the valuational focus that Hartmann accounts for the profound 'transvaluations' that occurred when the Greek world passed over into the Christian world, or the Christian world into the Renaissance world, and so on: all are by-products of an intense consciousness of new values whose swimming into the focus has pushed out the old. Such values are not really new, only hitherto ignored, and they are certainly not the creations of those who suddenly feel them, as Nietzsche thought them to be. This wandering of the value-focus, rather than malign resentment, is the cause of most value-errors and perversions, and it is these that the philosopher, with his balanced sympathy for all periods and societies, must therefore seek to correct. Hartmann has here certainly pointed out an important source of value-disputes. Nothing is more common than the assumption that if *A* and *B* exclude one another in practical realisation or in social cultivation, they necessarily exclude the possibility of each other's having value. This is plainly not the case: that *A* and *B* cannot both be does not mean that *A* and *B* cannot both be excellent. And though the impossible realisation of both sides of a contrary opposition might be the most valuable thing of all, it may still be the case, in this sorry, logical world, that realising one side of such an opposition may be better than realising nothing at all.

Hartmann's doctrine of the antinomic character of value comes out well in his treatment of what he calls the most elementary value-antitheses, an interesting, almost pre-Socratic collection of items. There is, he points out, a value in what must or should be the case (the law of nature or the holy will) but there is also a value in what may or may not be the case, the contingent, the variable and the free. There is an obvious value in the realisa-tion of values in the actual world, but there is also a value in their perpetual non-realisation, their essential transcendence of what is or can be. There is a value in moving *towards* valuable ends, and there is a value in desisting from movement in actual *achievement*. There is a value in constancy and uniformity, and a value in change and variety, a value in intensive purity and a value in many-sided richness, a value in harmonious poise and a value in exciting conflict, a value in simplicity and a value in complexity. There is a Kantian value in universality and a Schelerian value in individuality, there is a value in subordinating the individual to the community and a value in subordinating the community to the individual, and so on. To ordinary people all these antitheses involve homiletic truisms: only philosophers see them as para-doxes, or try to explain them away.

Above these pre-Socratic oppositions Hartmann ranges a series of values which lead up to and prepare the way for moral values. The most basic of these is the value of life, and above this the values of consciousness, of activity, of endurance, of power, of freedom, of foresight, of practical success: there are also supporting values of the environment with its many facilities and opportunities, values of the varying powers we dispose of, of the fortunate turn of occasions, of such social supports as friends, reputation, good birth, money, etc. Aristotle would have recognised all these as necessary ingredients of the good life: modern moral philosophers, concerned only with narrow, detailed problems of immediate duty, do not discuss them.

When we proceed to Moral Goodness, the summit of value in the Hartmannian scheme, the Schelerian principle is accepted that such moral value cannot be divorced from the pursuit of non-moral situational and goods-values, and in fact normally arises 'on the back' of this. Hartmann does not, however, accept the Schelerian exaggeration that the conscious pursuit of virtue is necessarily a case of corrupt Pharisaism. He rightly maintains that it is possible to cultivate virtue in oneself and in others, *provided* such cultivation goes with the committed, not merely instrumental cultivation of other goods. He also emphasises, as against any form of utilitarianism, that moral values do not, *qua* values, depend on the amount or degree of the lower values they realize or that they aim at: they are incomparably higher and better. The value of active justice in moral agents is, for example, much higher than the mere goods-value of the apportionments they effect.

In his treatment of moral values, Hartmann not only has a chapter on humdrum moral 'goodness', but on the more rarefied values of nobility, of *Fülle* or moral breadth, and of purity in its various contexts and senses. Unquestionably these are ethical modalities that merit attention and circumspection. Hartmann then discusses the characteristic ethical discoveries of the Hellenic world, of the Christian world and of that Germanic modernity which is represented by Nietzsche. He dwells at length on the four cardinal virtues of Plato's *Republic*, and gives an illuminating reinterpretation of Aristotle's doctrine of the Mean. He dwells on the specifically Christian discoveries of the value of neighbourly love, of humility, sincerity, fidelity and trust, and other great and deep virtues. He finds something to admire in Nietzsche's introduction of such new value as *Fernstenliebe* or Love of the Remote, and in *Schenkende Tugend* or Radiant Graciousness: the former contrasts with Neighbourly Love, without really discrediting it, and the latter with such Christian virtues as Humility. This part of the book has a richness and a truth to value-experience which renders it comparable to Aristotle's *Ethics* or Hegel's *Phenomenology of Spirit*. Hartmann does not write well. He in turn exhorts, sobs, spumes, pronounces, perorates, divagates and contradicts himself, and his work, even when well translated, gives small pleasure to Anglo-Saxon readers. But what he puts forth so poorly is often better worth meditating than the writings of far more lucid and temperate moralists. The firmament of values is not merely mapped in his writings: it springs up before us in remarkable, sparkling life.

V. FINAL SUGGESTIONS

We have now completed our short study of certain recent British and continental thinkers who have contributed importantly to the analysis of valuation and values, and who have also sketched an overall map of the value-firmament, of things good or bad in their order of hierarchical precedence or coordination, to the extent that any such order can be established among them. In the course of our study we have seen lively discussions arising in regard to questions upon which, according to certain opinions, only persuasion and not true discussion is possible, and we have also seen theorems winnowing themselves out which should be part of any well-considered treatment of value-issues: such as that there are radically different sorts or senses of value between which quantitative or even ordinal comparison is not readily possible, that there is a deep distinction between values that appear purely personal and those that claim cogency or validity, that values and disvalues have a close and necessary relation to feeling, but that the values which claim validity cannot be exhaustively analysed or even explained in terms of mere feeling, that the main 'heads' of impersonal, 'valid' valuation, freedom, fairness, happiness, etc., are moderately clear and quite readily agreed upon though their detailed specification or correct practical implementation is infinitely controversial, that value and disvalue have a close connection with various senses of 'ought', but that the central senses of the latter reveal it as a much more restricted conception, much more closely concerned with disvalues and their avoidance than with values, that values are not merely 'higher' than other values but also 'stronger', and that the 'strength' of value is connected with the disvalue of omitting something, that the values called 'moral' presuppose all other types of value as objects of pursuit, but that their value does not depend on the latter values, that moral value has a close connection with the readiness to sacrifice personal for impersonal good, etc. These and a large number of similar theorems can be said to have distilled themselves from the views we have examined, or they have remained over as a common precipitate. There is plainly 'something' in axiology as an analysis of soi-disant cogent valuation, and there is plainly 'something' in the systematic mapping of values and disvalues to which this analysis serves as a prelude.

Can we, however, get a better understanding of what is being done in all this elaborate value-cartography? Are there principles which explain how it is a possible and meaningful enterprise, one not merely based on a vague appeal to diffused, civilised sentiment? The way it has been conducted by the thinkers we have examined has not been very satisfactory. For Brentano, Meinong, Moore, Rashdall, Ross, Scheler and Hartmann have, in the main, appealed to intuition rather than argument. They have simply asked us to *agree* to such propositions as that knowledge is better than error, that readiness to make personal sacrifices increases merit, that enjoyment of beauty and personal affection are the highest of goods, that moral goodness excludes the deliberate pursuit of moral goodness and entails the pursuit of ends other than moral goodness, and so on. Some of these propositions are of great translucency, and there would certainly be great perversity in rejecting many of them. But philosophy is a tough game and a man should be allowed to espouse perverse positions if their perversity cannot be demonstrated or at least shown up as plausible. The emotivist theory that value-pronouncements merely register personal feelings and seek to impose it on others, may be a gross travesty of our value-experience, but it certainly fits many of the procedures of the philosophers we have been examining.

It is first necessary to clear out of the way any crassly 'objective' theory of values, such as is set up, for example, in Hartmann's account of the *ansichseiende*, self-existent value-world. It is not that such theories are demonstrably wrong: it is merely that it would not help us if they could be proved true. It is not illuminating to treat the ordering of values like the topography of the moon which can be established by simply training a telescope on one's object, or, more satisfactorily, by going there. The sort of values that one is concerned to establish in a systematic axiology are ineluctable, framework values, things presupposed in all rational choice, and indispensable to a complete account of anything whatever. The sort of 'objective' values in which some value-cartographers have believed have been merely empirical objects that we *find* to be there: they are in no sense framework conditions of possible existence or experience or endeavour. Such things as we find out there are by definition contingent, things that might also not have been there or that could be replaced by other things. Their relation to our feelings and desires is likewise contingent: it would be a mere fact of human nature that they appealed to us. Whereas a framework of cogent values cannot be a set of things that we merely happen to like or find inspiring: our liking or need of them must in some deep sense be necessary, and if there are no such objects of necessary liking or wanting then there are no such framework values at all.

This does not mean that to be necessarily liked or wanted is all that there is to being a cogent value: the emotivist analysis may have this amount of truth that it is only in feeling them, in being actually drawn to them, that we can fulfil or realise our understanding of what values are. They are not to be fully understood at a distance, in a framework of detached description: they must be experienced as making an actual impression on us for them to be fully there for us at all. But this need for direct emotional encounter does not mean that we cannot afterwards detachedly analyse what such encounter involves, and so frame an indirect characterisation, if not a true definition or description, of what such values are. Nor will it be wrong to attribute such values thus pinned down and characterised, to the framework of the universe. The mere 'seeing of values out there in things' is trivial: the most purely personal, the most superstitiously arbitrary values are quite readily seen 'out there'. The arguments of a phenomenology turned towards idealism are likewise inadequate: we cannot give values a place in the objective universe by the unacceptable ruse of arguing that the whole so-called objective universe has no more than an 'intentional inexistence' in our conscious references, and that the values perceived in it have therefore as secure a place in the objective universe as any other part of its structure. We may concede the metaphysical transcendence of the natural world as what our references to it always imply and sometimes see, or claim to see, with assurance, but this does not mean that we need regard it as an external accident that this world declares itself to our perception and judgement, or that in a still more intimate encounter it declares what it is to our emotions. To feel about something may in certain privileged cases be the last, most penetrating way of knowing what the thing is, and what stands before us as the 'objective correlate' of such feelings may be in truth the very 'nucleus' of the things themselves.

It is not, however, our task in the concluding chapter of this monograph, to make out a case for all these murkily stated contentions. What will be suggested is that we do require something like the Transcendental Deduction of Kant to show why value-research and value-cartography should be possible, why it is not nonsensical to set up a framework of 'heads of value' within which our emotional endeavours and practical responses can be channelled, in so far, that is, as they can come to have the authority and internal correctness which some of them are certainly experienced as having. Kant tried to show, with very imperfect success, that there are certain framework conditions of what can be brought home to perception and judgement as objective, as having the kind of being that can be successfully investigated and established, and he also tried, with still smaller success, to show that there are certain framework conditions, certain categorial limitations, in what can be recommended as a possible line of action to someone who not only acts, but also reflects rationally on how he should act. If Kant's transcendental broodings on morality only led him to the empty puritanical formalisms that have been so often criticised, is it arguable that a more penetrating transcendentalism will establish something like that rich tapestry of values that we have studied in the philosophers of our choice, and so rescue us from the mere dogmatism and intuitionism which these philosophers have practised? It is a belief in the possibilities of such a transcendentalism that has inspired the present writer to produce his *Values and Intentions*, as well as many papers on Ethics such as 'The Methodology of Normative Ethics', 'The Structure of the Kingdom of Ends' and others. All these writings had their source in the axiological thinkers we have studied, and have sought to find a rational basis for their intuitive conclusions. The contents of these writings will not here be set forth, but we shall try to set forth the line of transcendental explanation they contain in supplementation and criticism of the philosophers in question.

The kind of transcendentalism we are trying to expound is one that has roots in the moral philosophy of the eighteenth century, and particularly in the ethical writings of Adam Smith, which have had important modern echoes in Meinong's discussion of the moral value-subject in his *Psychological-Ethical Investigations into Value-Theory*, as well as in Scheler's important work on the *Essence of Sympathy* (*Das Wesen der Sympathie*). It lays stress on the fact that to be a conscious experient is not merely to have commerce with objects, but also to have commerce with other subjects, into whose subjective approaches one sympathetically enters, and in association with whom one not only establishes an acceptable view of the world but also arrives at acceptable practical ways of coping with that world. Such sympathetic entry is not merely some curious psychological capacity which human organisms happen to have, and which rests precariously on a more basic relation to physical objects: it is a capacity that conscious thinking beings cannot be without, if they are to be confronted with any objects at all. Through the caprices of a stepmotherly nature one might indeed be stranded in a situation without fellows *with* whom one could face, and could act on, nature, but the *place* for such fellows would always be present: it is a categorial, a necessary place. And it is categorial not merely in its observable physical aspects but also in its unobservable, interior aspects: through sympathy, which is not necessarily based on one's own personal experiences, one enters into the not straightforwardly observable inner life of others, which always has a necessary place in our world, though its precise content may be filled in, often with grave need of correction, by experience, imagination or inference. This necessary being-with-others, and with others *given* from the first as having an *ungiven* dimension as well as a straightforwardly given one, is something for which we shall not here argue. The use of personal pronouns in language, with its unmysterious though deeply metaphysical passage from 'I' to 'you' and vice versa, nothing being more evident than the at least partial secrecy of what 'you' experience to what 'I' experience and vice versa, is evidence for it, as is also the strange fact of Wittgenstein's conversion, in the course of his philosophical development, from an exaggeratedly solipsistic theory of meaning to an exaggeratedly public one. We are not concerned to defend this last, nor to maintain more than the necessary presence of a possible public dimension to the possibility of object-directed experience and of language in the full sense of the word. Fellows and objects are necessary to one another, and it is only in relation to both that we ourselves can be subjects and can make significant references to things, people and our own mental and bodily life.

All this being presupposed, the entry into other people's, and into other sentient beings', feelings and interests is a necessary part of our experience of a possible world and of our ability to talk significantly and testably about it. It is important not to understress the metaphysical oddity of the sympathetic performance. For it is in a sense the divesting of ourselves of the specificity of our interest and our conscious content and the particularity of our person, and the imagining ourselves in a position that is, on many views, totally unimaginable, and because thus unimaginable, also totally unmeaning. How can Octavius imagine what it would be like if *he*, Octavius, were Cleopatra, and how can a convinced Nazi put *himself* into the shoes of a hounded Jew, all performances recommended by certain modern metamoralists, and yet involving an apparent logical absurdity that would make the endeavour quite vain? We shall not dwell on this point, for the absurdity plainly has its roots more in current concepts of personal identity, and of identity generally, and of the so-called 'criteria' of the same, than in anything in the undoubted performance which we all can and very often do carry out. The sort of sameness possible for a person is plainly not a sameness that excludes the *possibility* of being in *some* sense quite a different person. Obviously, however, the beings who often perform whatever may be meant by putting themselves into other people's shoes, and who have acquired some skill and zest in this performance, must in the end tend to move to a new, higher level of interest where what they concern themselves with is not what this one or that one likes or is interested in, but only with what *survives* all such laborious translation of oneself into everyone else's shoes, so that one then, at that level, only desires and likes what everyone must desire and like, and desire and like for everyone, and desire and like everyone to desire and like for everyone, and so in unending complication. Such beings, who are of course ourselves, must become concerned with the new, higher-order objects of interest of what Adam Smith called the impartial spectator but who is better described as the impartial judge or agent: the man who desires not to want or like for anyone, at least in his impartial capacity, what he cannot want or like for all. The logical structure of such impartiality is much more teasingly complex than the above characterisations might suggest, and much care is required if one is to avoid inconsistency and circularity and to achieve fruitfulness. All this cannot, however, be argued in this place. But what must be stressed is that some rising to this impartial standpoint is not only involved in all practical cooperation but also in the developed form of the discourse which goes with it. Without some rising to invariances of aim which are unaffected by the specificity of personal interest or the particularity of persons, it would not be possible to consult or advise or plan in concert. Practical discourse of this developed sort can have purchase and sense only if it is in some sense addressed *to anyone* and prescribes *for anyone*, even if that *anyone* is at first merely anyone in some limited group, or anyone having some property, or anyone conceived in this sheer separate particularity. To counsel is to suggest what anyone in a given position should do: it is to tell a man what anyone in his position should do, not merely what I want him to do or what someone else wants him to do or what he himself wants to do. I must to some extent put him into the position of anyone, or anyone into his position, if I am to advise and not merely to hector or defer. And from the *anyone* of the tribe or the *anyone* of the conspiratorial conclave or the *anyone* concerned solely with that anyone himself, we progress to the anyone concerned with anyone by the same unlimited freeing of variables which we also encounter in the sphere of logic, and which makes it natural to say that the wholly free variable is *implicit* in the restricted one. We may say therefore that without some implicit relation to the total body of possible persons, whether as agents, patients or judges, practical discourse would not make sense: one cannot significantly ask what one ought, or what it would be reasonable to do. And the *impersonal authority* of the interests which pursue only what everyone must desire for everyone is quite unmysterious: it is merely a consequence of what impersonal interests as such are. In them speaks the voice of Everyman addressing himself to Everyman, beside which the voices of particular interests belonging to particular persons necessarily shrink back, as not having the unboundedly general appeal that is in question. And if they do not shrink back, they do so only as being the powerful personal interests that they are and not as involving anything like an impersonal 'authority'.

What we have, however, to show is that – this exalted higher-order interest in what anyone could and would find interesting for anyone having been formed – it must of necessity generate just such a system of higher-order values as Moore, Ross, Scheler, Hartmann, etc., have sketched for us so elaborately. It seems possible, *prima facie*, that there are *no* universal objects which conform to the requirements in question, that what everyone could or would desire for everyone is an emptily unspecifiable notion. It is arguable, however, that such is not the case, and that while, no doubt, we can play about with 'logical possibilities' which are not genuine possibilities at all, there in fact are, and must be, higher-order objects which satisfy the condition of being what everyone could or would desire for everyone, and would desire everyone to desire for everyone, and so on.

It is arguable, first of all, that the traditional hedonic goals of universal pleasure and happiness are in this condition. They ignore, without overriding or eliminating, the specificity of personal interest and the particularity of the person. They involve in short, that everyone, no matter who he may be, should have whatever he likes or wants, whatever this last may be – clashes of interest of course involve complications, which we need not here consider – and that he should want everyone to have the same. Universal malevolence, though logically consistent if higher-order interest be separated from lower-order interest, would involve an uncomfortable policy of self-frustration at lower levels, and, if carried up to higher levels, would involve a yet more uncomfortable malevolence towards one's own malevolence, and malevolence towards this second malevolence, and so on indefinitely. In a similar manner, if one attempts to answer Adam Smith's difficulty as to why one should sympathise with the victims of aggression and not with the aggressors, the answer lies in the fact it would be infinitely uncomfortable and rent with conflicts to sympathise with all aggressors, whereas sympathising with those who do not aggress, would if all adopted such a stance, involve no internal discrepancy or conflict. A conflict of inner attitudes does not involve a logical contradiction, but it does involve the same sort of inner disquiet that a contradiction does in those who try to accept it. It is arguable, likewise, that the goals of power and freedom are goals which ignore specificity of first-order interest and personal particularity, and are accordingly goals that (with due restrictions for conflict) can and would be desired by everyone for everyone.

Having argued all this, it is not hard to see a track of argument leading to the valuation of impartial justice, to evade which must involve difficult perversity. For the whole self-divestment of the particularity and specificity of interest has nothing partial about it, and partiality could only be added to it by some wanton, extrinsic addition. In the pursuit of impartial justice we merely set up as a conscious aim what is already followed in principle, we make into a new, higher-order goal what is already involved in the impartial pursuit of lower goals. Such an erection of impartiality into a higher-order aim of course results in many refinements: it is one thing to be unbiased in one's treatment of persons, it is another more scrupulous thing to pursue lack of bias as an end in itself. What it is important to note is that the development of this new, higher-order interest is in a sense logical and inevitable, though not so in a purely formal sense. There is a step involved in passing from merely acting in accordance with a principle and making an end of that principle, and it is a step that it would be possible not to take, and one that one is not compelled to take. There is nothing formally inconsistent in being indifferent to differences of person and character of interest, without erecting such indifference into a conscious end. But to take this step is, in a quite ordinary sense, 'natural', 'logical' and 'consistent'. It would be odd and strange not to esteem a principle that one already follows in one's estimations.

It is not necessary to explain how a tendency to rise above the specificity and particularity of interest should lead one on to valuing that imperfect but more intense rising above the specificity and particularity of interest which is involved in the deeper forms of unselfish personal love. The step in question could, with formal consistency, be evaded: it remains, however, deeply consequent. In a similar manner it is not hard to follow Kant in the *Critique of Judgement* when he recognises a profound homology between aesthetic and ethical disinterestedness, so that the beautiful becomes in necessary fashion a 'monogram' of the good. In both aesthetic and properly axiological interest there is a rising above the specificity and particularity of first-order interest: arguably, therefore, in virtue of such an affinity, aesthetic interest and its objects become of concern to our 'practical' value-interests. And the same applies to the disinterestedness of the cognitive sphere, and the various values that develop from it, values so richly recognised by Kant in his consideration of regulative principles at the end of the *Critique of Pure Reason*. The last stone in the arch is of course the moral value or virtue of pursuing all these variously specified values: it would be inconceivably perverse and in a deep sense inconsequent to value certain ends and not to value the will which bends itself to realise these, and which in a sense comprises them all in its intentions. Our valuations of the good will must, however, be Schelerian rather than Kantian: it will presuppose all the lower values which give it content and meaning, while not exhaustively depending for its value on these last. What we see emerging in all this is an organised body of values, the authentic membership of the Absolute Good. And it is plain that all these members are to be found recognised and honourably mentioned somewhere or other in the writings of Kant: only his official pronouncements on Ethics reveal the restrictive impress of his pietistic forebears.

One comment is necessary on the whole method of our undertaking: that it throughout exploits a loose logic of analogy or affinity, similar to the logic of inductive arguments, and not at all a rigorous formal pattern of deduction such as some philosophers would alone consider 'logical'. Sometimes this logic works simply by extending to a case B an attitude already directed to a *closely similar* case A; sometimes it takes on a wider sweep, and generalises an emotional attitude confined at first to a limited class of cases. This last is illustrated by the passage from the limited benignity and limited impartiality which follows from close entry into the interests of certain others, to the wider benignity and impartiality which is extended to all sentient beings, etc. It is a well-known fact that there is no easy way of formalising analogical arguments, or distinguishing on paper between a profound and relevant resemblance and one superficial and of small relevance. All this of course applies *a fortiori* to the resemblances relevant to valuational attitudes.

But the kind of analogy which is most important for cogent value-formation is not, however, entirely an ordinary movement along lines of resemblance: it is also what Ehrenfels calls a movement *inwards*, a movement from valuing an object X towards valuing the attitude which values X. This is not an ordinary case of analogy since the valuation of X does not resemble X at all. This movement is illustrated by the transition from being impartial to valuing impartiality as such, or from being benign to being concerned with benignity, or from being concerned with certain good objectives to being concerned with one's own or with other people's concern for them. Plainly it is in a deep sense 'natural' and 'consistent' to like the liking of X if one likes X: even at the level of purely personal taste we behold, for example, ardent fishers liking other ardent fishers. This elementary tendency is, of course, exploited to the full in Stevenson's emotivistic analyses of value-judgements. What does not, however, appear at the Stevensonian level is the *logical* character of the move from favouring X to favouring the favouring of X. It is not a logical move in the sense of an obligatory entailment – one need not take it, and may even *refuse* to take it – but it is none the less 'reasonable' in the paradigmatic sense in which inductive and analogical arguments are 'reasonable'. It is thus by a loose logic of straightforward analogy combined with the 'movement inward' just examined, that the whole firmament of values necessarily arises, and builds up its form and its force: it is, in fact, as inconceivable that the pattern of 'highest heads' of value set up by ourselves will not arise in every reflective society as that men in such societies will not develop a largely similar number-system or a calculus of probabilities.

It is obvious from our arguments that the 'highest heads' of value are not only established by an exceedingly lax if all-important logic, but that they are also exceedingly vague in outline and content. To seek happiness, freedom and opportunity for all, and to be impartial in seeking them, and to value the attitudes involved in such seeking and in such impartiality, and also to value certain cognitive, aesthetic and affectionate attitudes having some affinity with the attitudes just mentioned, all yield unexceptionable, copybook ideals from which hardly any well-thinking person would dissent, but it remains infinitely hard to say what these ideals mean in the concrete, and particularly so in the many cases in which their claims conflict with one another. Here the wrong approach is to hold, as the philosophers of our choice all hold, that there is some one correct implementation of all the values in question in each concrete case, and that the difficulty of arriving at such a correct result is merely like that of determining, from simple physical principles, the course that a stone will take as it bounds down some complicated hillside. But the two difficulties are not alike since the laws which govern the movement of stones are not vague, nor are the contours of the most complicated hillside, whereas in the realm of values everything has blurred edges: mist is as much part of the picture as in a Chinese painting. It is absurd to drag in an Aristotelian perception αἴσθησις, to solve one problem, for such αἴσθησις is useless where there is nothing to perceive. Plainly a cutting of the Gordian knot after full contemplation of all values and disvalues present or possible in a situation, is all that remains open to the practical agent: it is a decision, not insight, that is required. Yet in a sense the doctrine of αἴσθησις makes sense, since a conscientious decision among incompatible value-claims is always felt to be right for the individual in question, and felt to be right not by that individual alone but by all who consider his case. For them, otherwise oriented and circumstanced, another decision might have been correct, but his decision, representing the deepest response of his practical being, is right for him, and, as limited to him, right for all. The doctrines of vocation on which Rashdall and Scheler have laid such stress here come into their full right. We are not free to determine the points of the compass in the realm of values, but remain free, within wide limits, to steer a course among them.

We have now come to the end of suggesting ways of improving axiological ethics by giving it something like a transcendental deduction to rest on. It is not maintained that these ways are mandatory, but only that they are suggestive. There really is, it would seem, an organised framework of values and disvalues within which our practical decisions must be made, and philosophy must give some account of the structure of this framework and of the principles guiding its construction. A transcendental deduction need not, further, be regarded as the last word in the matter. It may only be a first step leading to a metaphysical deduction that is far more profound and far-reaching. For the self-transcendence of consciousness involved in our intentional references, and the further self-transcendence of consciousness in the sympathetic entry into the inner life of others, are amazing, paradoxical performances: though they form the very warp and woof of our conscious existence, we must still ask how they are possible. Possibly in reference to a Unity which, like the Platonic Good or Neoplatonic One, transcends Being and Knowledge, and yet necessarily gives rise to both and draws them back from their imperfection to its more than perfect self? Whatever we may decide on such ultimate issues, the construction of a value-firmament remains a worthwhile, and not impracticable, philosophical task.

BIBLIOGRAPHY

Brentano, F. *Vom Ursprung sittlicher Erkenntnis* (1889). Trans. Roderick Chisholm, as *The Origin of Our Knowledge of Right and Wrong* (1969).

Dewey, J. *Theory of Valuation* (Chicago, 1939).

Eaton, H. O. *The Austrian Theory of Values* (Oklahoma, 1930).

Ehrenfels, Chr. von. *System der Werttheorie* (*System of Value-Theory*) 2 vols (Leipzig, 1897–8).

Ewing, A. C. *The Definition of Good* (Cambridge, 1947).

Findlay, J. N. *Meinong's Theory of Objects and Values* (Oxford, 1963).

——, *Language, Mind and Value* (1963).

——, *Values and Intentions* (1961).

Hartmann, N. *Ethik* (Berlin, 1926). Trans. Stanton Coit, as *Ethics*, 3 vols (1932).

Laird, J. *The Idea of Value* (Cambridge, 1961).

Lepley, R. *Value: A Co-operative Inquiry* (New York, 1952).

Lewis, C. I. *An Analysis of Knowledge and Valuation* (La Salle, Illinois, 1946).

Meinong, A. *Psychologisch-ethische Untersuchungen zur Werththeorie* (*Psychological-Ethical Investigations into Value-Theory*) (Graz, 1894).

——, *Über emotionale Präsentation* (*On Emotional Presentation*) (Vienna, 1917).

——, *Zur Grundlegung der allgemeinen Werttheorie* (*Foundations of General Value-Theory*) (Graz, 1932).

——, *Ethische Bausteine* (*Ethical Building-Stones*) (Graz, 1969). All republished in vol. III of Meinong's *Gesamtausgabe* (Collected Works) (Graz, 1969).

Moore, G. E. *Principia Ethica* (Cambridge, 1903).

Perry, R. B. *General Theory of Value* (New York, 1926).

Rashdall, H. *The Theory of Good and Evil*, 2 vols (Oxford, 1907).

Ross, W. D. *The Right and the Good* (Oxford, 1930).
——, *The Foundations of Ethics* (Oxford, 1939).
Scheler, Max. *Der Formalismus in der Ethik und die materiale Wertethik (Formalism in Ethics and the Material Value-Ethic)* (Halle, 1916).
Stevenson, C. L. *Ethics and Language* (New Haven, 1944).
Urban, W. *Valuation: Its Nature and Laws* (1906).
Wright, G. H. von. *The Varieties of Goodness* (1963).